Fennec Fox

Fennec Fox pet

Fennec Fox keeping, care, housing, training, diet and health.

By

George Galloway

ALL RIGHTS RESERVED. This book contains material protected under International and Federal Copyright Laws and Treaties.

Any unauthorized reprint or use of this material is strictly prohibited. No part of this book may be reproduced or transmitted in any form or by any means, electronic, mechanical or otherwise, including photocopying or recording, or by any information storage and retrieval system without express written permission from the author.

Copyright © 2017

Published by: IMB Publishing

Table of Contents

Introduction 4

Chapter 1: Understanding a Fennec Fox 6

Chapter 2: Understanding the Animal in its Natural Habitat 16

Chapter 3: Things you Need to Know before Purchasing 26

Chapter 4: Purchasing the Fennec Fox 41

Chapter 5: Diet Requirements 54

Chapter 6: Training the Fennec Fox 61

Chapter 7: Ideal environment for the Fennec Fox 65

Chapter 8: Common Health Issues 70

Chapter 9: Necessary Precautions to be Taken 75

Conclusion 80

References 82

Introduction

I want to thank you and congratulate you for buying the book 'Fennec fox as a pet'. This book will help you to understand everything you need to know about domesticating a fennec fox. You will learn all the aspects related to raising the fennec fox successfully at home. You will be able to understand the pros and cons, basic care, keeping, housing, diet and health related to the fennec fox.

The fennec foxes have always been popular as the wild, naughty and good looking foxes. People liked them but were scared to raise them at home. But, slowly things started changing and people started domesticating them and raising them at home. Raising an exotic animal is not all fun. There is a lot of hard work that goes into it. It is important that you are ready to commit before you decide to domesticate the animal. One of the most important factors that make the fennec fox so popular is the exotic looks of the animal. The fennec is small in size and has large ears. It has a cute face that makes people fall in love with him. But, before you go and buy the fennec for his looks, it is important that you know that the cost of bringing up a fox is more than the cost you would have to encounter while raising an ordinary pet.

If you are looking to domesticate the fennec fox, then you might be having many questions and doubts. You still might not be sure whether you want to buy the fennec or not. If you are still doubtful, then you can relax because this book is meant to help you make a well-informed decision. When you decide to domesticate an animal, it is important that you understand the animal and its species well. It is important to learn the basic nature and mannerisms of the animal. This book will help you to equip yourself with this knowledge. You will be able to appreciate the fennec for what they are. You will also know what to expect from the animal. This will help you to decide whether the fennec fox is the right choice for you or not.

You should know that the requirements of your pet fennec fox will be very different from the requirements of your pet cat or dog. You can't expect to face similar challenges when domesticating two entirely different pets. Domesticating an exotic animal can be a very pleasant experience if you are prepared with what you can expect and what not to expect. You need to know about the responsibilities that lay ahead of you. It is important to have a thorough understanding about the animal. Spend some time to know more about the fennec fox. This will help you know your pet better. The more you know about your pet, the better bond you will form with him.

Whenever you bring a pet home, you have to make sure that you are all ready for the responsibilities ahead. A pet is like a family member. The pet should not be your status symbol. You should love him and care for him deeply. This is the basic requirement to domesticate an animal. There is a certain life style that the fennec fox is accustomed to. When you bring the animal home, you disturb that natural way of living. So, it is more than important that you take care of all the responsibilities for the fennec fox.

It can get very daunting for a new owner. You might be confused and scared. But, you don't need to be scared. No matter how scared you are, you can always make it work if you equip yourself with the right knowledge. If you understand how a fennec fox should be cared for, you will make it work for yourself. You should aim to learn about the animal and then do the right thing for him. This will help you to form a relationship with him. Once you form a relationship with the fennec fox, it gets better and easier for you as the owner. The pet will grow up to be friendly and adorable. He will also value the bond as much as you do.

This book is meant to equip you with all the knowledge that you need to have before buying the fennec fox and bringing it home. This book is an attempt to list all the important reference points for understanding the fennec fox in a better light. These points can be a quick guide when you are looking for some specific information about the fennec fox. You will learn about the fennec fox's basic temperaments, eating habits, natural habitat, shelter requirements, breeding and mating patterns and other important things. This book will address every question that you might have when looking at raising the fennec fox. You will be able to understand the pet and give it the care that it requires. This will help you form an everlasting bond with your fennec fox.

Chapter 1: Understanding a Fennec Fox

The word fennec has being derived from another word that is Arabic in its origin, 'fanak'. The word 'fanak' literally means a fox. The scientific name of the fennec fox is the 'VulpesZerda'. The fennec fox belongs to Canid or Canidae. The Canidae is the biological term used to denote the group of wolves, foxes, coyotes, jackals and some domestic dogs.

A male fennec fox is referred to as a 'Reynard', whereas the female fennec fox is often called a 'vixen'. The young ones are referred to as pup, kit or cub. You might also be interested to know what a group of fennec foxes is called. They are often referred as 'skulk' or 'leash'. The fennec fox can also be called as a fennec.

There was a time when people would hesitate to domesticate exotic animals. The main reason for this was that not much information was available about these animals. There were too many doubts in the minds of the people, and there was no source to clear these doubts. But, in today's world, with so much information available, it is becoming easier for people to learn more about exotic animals and domesticate them. Like many other exotic animals, the fennec foxes are also slowly becoming the most sought after pets. They look very adorable and sweet. They have small bodies and large ears, making their appearance extremely lovable to the current and also the prospective owners. Their ears are their most defining feature.

Fennec foxes are known to be nocturnal in nature. This makes them very active at the night time. A potential owner should definitely consider this point before deciding to buy the animal. Like the other foxes, the fennec fox is also considered to be very agile, witty and wise.

1. Taxonomy

It is interesting to note that the fennec foxes have many characteristics that make them differ from other foxes. In spite of being from the same family, there are many traits that totally separate the fennec fox from other foxes. Scientists had to consider many factors before they could categorise fennec foxes. The differences that the fennecs exhibited have led to much confusion while the scientists tried to classify and name them. If you do a careful study, you will realize that the characteristics that separate a fennec fox from other foxes are not just physical, but also social.

If you study the DNA of the fennec fox and the other foxes, you will find a very vital difference there also. The fennec fox is known to have 32 chromosome pairs in its DNA strand. In comparison to this, the other foxes have either 35 chromosome pairs or 39 chromosomes pairs in their DNA strand. The physical features distinguish the fennec fox from other foxes. Apart from this, the fennec foxes exhibit a very characteristic social behaviour. The fennec like being in groups and are mostly found in the company of other fennecs. The other foxes don't like being in groups. They like being alone and can usually be spotted all alone.

Because of the various differences that the fennec fox exhibits when compared to other foxes, many scientists believe that the fennec fox needs to have a separate genus. These scientists want the fox to have the genus 'Fennecus'. These scientists have also changed the scientific name of the fennec fox. The scientific name is identified as 'FennecusZerda'. There have been many studies and researches for identifying these differences. According to a latest study on the foxes, scientists have decided to club the fennec fox and all the other foxes under the common classification 'Vulpes'.

Scientific Classification

If you are looking to understand the Scientific Classification of the fennec fox, then the following will be of a great help to you:

Common name of Fennecs: Fennec fox

Kingdom of Fennecs: The Animalia

Phylum of Fennecs: The Chordata

Class of Fennecs: The Mammalia

Family of Fennecs: The Canidae

Order of Fennecs: The Carnivora

Genus of Fennecs: The Vulpes

Species of Fennecs: The Zerda, which mean the small in Arabic.

2. Physical appearance of the fennec fox

The fennec fox belongs to the class Canidae. This makes their physical appearance quite similar to other members of this class, such as wolves, foxes, coyotes, jackals and some domestic dogs. The members of the class have many common characteristics.

It is known that the fennec foxes belong to the smallest species of the fox class. The most striking feature of a fennec fox is definitely its ears. As compared to the small body of the fox, the ears are relatively very big. The ears are actually bat-like in appearance. Even the tail of the fox makes it stand apart from most other animals. The fennec is very small in appearance. In comparison to the body of the fox, the tail is quite long.

When it comes to the physical appearance of the fennec, it has a bushy tail and claws that are non-retractile in nature. The fennec fox is able to walk on its claws, just like other members of the class Canidae. Another striking feature of the fox is the thumb like claw, known as the dewclaw. This dewclaw is similar to the thumb of the human. It is called the dog's thumb. This dewclaw never touches the floor when the fox is standing on its legs.

The fox has a covering of a thick and soft fur around it. The fur is cream or fawn in colour. The fur that covers the stomach area of the fennec fox is white in colour. The tail is of a similar cream colour, while the tip is bushy and black. The colour of the fur of the fox helps it in many ways. The desert sand is also of a similar colour. This allows the fennec fox to hide himself from its predators. The colour of the fur blends in well with the colour of the desert sand. The anal glands of the fennec fox are coated with some dark bristles. The paws of the fennec fox also give the necessary protection. The base or sole of the paws are covered with fur to protect them and give them the necessary grip.

Body measurements

The fennec fox is considered to be the smallest Canidae in the entire world. This makes the animal very small and petite in appearance. It is known that as an adult, the fennec fox does not weight more than 2 to 3.5 pounds. The weight of the younger fennec fox is obviously even lesser than the average weight of the adult fox. If you measure the fennec lengthwise, the measurements wouldn't be more than 23 – 41 cms. The height of an adult fennec fox is around 20 cm. The tail of a fennec fox is very tall in comparison to the body. The average length is about 18 – 30 cms. As discussed earlier, the ears are a peculiar feature of the fennec foxes. The average length is 8 – 15 cms.

The structure of the legs and paws of the fennec render it the strength of being a very fast runner. The fennec darts from one place to another very quickly. While this skill is helpful for the fox in the desert to escape other dangerous animals, the new owners struggle to keep track of the fox. In its natural habitat, the fennec runs and jumps from a sand dune to another sand dune to protect itself. The fennec can reach a running speed of 20 mph. Another point to be noted here is that the fennec will not just run fast, but will also change directions and switch routes very quickly. This is also a way to protect itself. When a fox jumps, it can reach to a height of 2 feet, which is absolutely incredible. The distance that it can cover in one jump is almost 4 feet.

3. Adaptations to survive in the Desert

The fennec fox has evolved well over the years. The animal has changes in its behaviour and lifestyle patterns so that it can survive. These adaptations allow him to live in conditions that are otherwise very harsh and drastic. These adaptations allow the fennec to live a healthy and long life in the extreme environment of the desert. In the absence of these adaptations, the fox might not have survived for too long. It might have just gone extinct.

Natural habitat

The fennec fox is naturally found in the Sahara Desert. Their range extends from the desert regions of North Africa to those of the Arabian Peninsula. Owing to their desert environment, the fennec fox is used to a low water environment. They can thrive very well in such areas. The fox can even live for days without drinking water. The days in the desert are very humid and hot. The nights, on the other hand, can be very cold. Over the years, the fennec has adapted so well to such extreme conditions. The fennecs dig burrows and spend time resting in those burrows. The fox is very agile and can dig very deep burrows in a short amount of time.

Physical adaptations

As mentioned, the days in the desert are very hot, while the nights are relatively cooler. A physical adaptation that helps the fennec to deal with this change of day and night is its fur colour. If you notice, the colour of the fox's fur is very light. This light colour will reflect away the heat during the hot day time. The fur is also very thick. This helps the fennec to keep itself warmer during the cold nights.

The paws of the fennec fox are also suitably adapted to the desert environment. The paws are padded with lots of soft fur. This gives the fox the freedom to roam on the very hot sands. In fact, the animal is very agile on these hot sands too. These paws are also well suited to dig deep burrows. These burrows help the fennec store food and make escape routes. They also help the animal to hide and protect himself in case of any danger.

It should also be noted that just like how the fur coated paws enable the fennec to walk freely on the hot sand, they also enable him to walk on snow and ice. The paws provide the necessary grip to walk on snow without sliding away.

To be able to run away from danger, the animal should be able to jump and run very fast. The hind legs of the fox are very strong. These legs allow him to jump to great heights. The fennec fox can easily lift itself off the ground and jump to a height of two feet to about a meter. This helps the fox not just to save himself from predators, but also to pounce on its prey.

Lifestyle and behavioural adaptations

The fennec fox has adapted itself very well to the extreme weather conditions in the desert. They can survive and thrive even in the most extreme conditions. The breathing rate of the fox in a normal environment is about 23-24 breaths in a minute. On the other hand, they can show a drastic change in their breathing in different circumstances. They can take around 690-700 breaths in a single minute when their body is overheating. This is just a simple example to prove how well they adapt to their circumstances.

The fennec fox saves all his excess food deep inside the burrows. This ensures that the family of the fox has food in times of need. The burrow also helps to save the food from other animals in the region. The nocturnal behaviour of the fennec fox is also an adaptation to survive well in the humid desert. The desert sun can be almost unbearable in the day time. The fox utilizes the hot day by resting and restoring its energy. At the night time, when it is relatively cooler, it ventures out. This adaptation helps the fox to survive well in hot and humid desert areas.

Another lifestyle and behavioural adaptation that can be observed in the fennec foxes is their ability to reproduce as per the circumstances. It is important for the fox that the family is thriving. They reproduce and have one litter every year. One litter per year ensures that there is no scarcity of food and the family line also keeps growing. But, there are times when there is abundance of food or when most of the litters have died due to unpleasant circumstances, then the fennec fox can reproduce twice a year.

4. Important points to understand

Raising an exotic animal is not all fun. There is a lot of hard work that goes into it. It is important that you are ready to commit before you decide to domesticate the animal. If you wish to raise a fennec fox as a pet, there are many things that you need to keep in mind. You can't just go and bring the animal home. Before you can do that, you need to make sure that you are ready in terms of preparation. You need to be a hundred per cent sure before you do this.

Unlike earlier times, many people have started domesticating fennec foxes now. But, there is only limited understanding amongst potential owners regarding the domestication of these animals. So, it is important to be acquainted with the dos and don'ts of keeping a fennec fox as a pet. This will help you to be a good owner and will also make sure that your pet is happy in your home. What is the use of bringing an animal home if he is not happy? You should make sure that you understand the requirements of the fennec fox in the best possible way.

Fennec foxes are unlike most other foxes. But, there are some basic traits that they share with the foxes. They can be as ferocious and dangerous as them. What qualities the fennec fox exhibits depends a lot on the kind of domestication it is given. The fennec foxes can be raised to be social and less aggressive, and they can also turn out to be ferocious and non-social if not raised the right way. Fennec foxes are very entertaining, adorable and lovable animals. But, they should not be deprived of all that they would have found in their natural habitat. You have to take care of their food requirements, along with other basic requirements. They have certain specific requirements that need to be met.

Before you buy a fennec fox, you should make sure that you are fully prepared for the responsibility ahead. You have to understand their specific requirements before you can buy them. This will serve you and the fennec fox in the long run.

You should also be sure that you and your family will be able to make sure that the animal is happy and safe at your place. If there is a slightest possibility that the animal will not be taken care of in the right way in your household, it is always better to not domesticate the animal. This does not mean that you should be scared about domesticating a fennec fox. You just need to be a little cautious.

There are many points that you should consider when you are looking to buy and domesticate a fennec fox. When you are considering keeping a fennec fox as a pet, you should lay special emphasis on the following few points:

Cost: It is very practical to consider the financial aspects of keeping a fennec fox. You can't buy one without giving a clear thought towards this aspect. A fennec fox will definitely cost you more than a regular pet. You will also have to spend more money to raise it in comparison to raising other pets. The exotic animal will come with a price, and you should be ready and prepared to pay the price. You should understand the various expenditures that you will have to incur in different stages of growth of the fennec fox. This cost estimation will help you to decide whether you can afford to keep this exotic animal or not.

Licensing requirements: You have to understand the licensing requirements in your area before you can keep a fennec fox. This is important so that you can avert any future issues and problems. You should make sure that you understand the related legal aspect before you go ahead and buy the animal. As a prospective buyer, you will have to buy a fennec fox from a legally certified fennec breeder. The USDA governs the rules binding the domestication of exotic animals, such as fennec foxes in the United States of America. So, make sure that you understand the rules of your state before you buy the fennec fox. You might get certain options to buy the fennec fox illegally, but you should not give in to such means and ways. It is extremely important that you go about the entire process of buying and domesticating a fennec fox the legal way. This could be a little costlier, but it is important. You should be able to appreciate the fact that we are talking about an exotic pet here. The rules that bound it will be very different from the rules for other pet animals. It is illegal to domesticate a fennec fox by capturing him from the wild. This is a punishable offence. Only certified fennec breeders can do so.

Compatibility issues: Do you have another pet at home? If yes, then you would also have to look into the compatibility between your pet and fennec fox. It is important that all your pets can live harmoniously with each other. There are many studies that are being done to understand the relationship of fennec foxes with other animals in the wild. These studies have proven that the fennecs are cordial towards each other and like hanging out in groups. So, if you have another fennec at home, then the fennecs will get along. It is also important to understand what kind of a relationship your fennec will have with the other pets in the house. This will help you to plan well and also in advance. Their relationship with other kinds of animals will depend on many factors. A point to be noted here is that they will kill and eat any animal that is smaller in size that them.

Diet requirements: What will the pet eat? What should I feed the pet? This can be the biggest concern while looking to get a pet. You have to make sure that you understand the diet requirements of the fennec fox before you can decide to domesticate it. By nature, the fennec fox is omnivorous. The animal can eat both plants and animal based food. It is important that the food that you give to your pet gives it proper nourishment. The fennec fox should be given cat food once or twice a day. The food should be good quality. This canned cat food should be wet and it will form as a base to its food requirements. The fennec fox requires a diet that is high in taurine. Many fennec fox owners feed their foxes only with canned cat food or dog food. It is important to give other food with the canned foods. You can also look to give them pills to supplement the nutrients that the food is not providing them.

Space constraints: A fennec fox is an active animal. This makes it important that you have enough space for the pet. The space that you give him should be enough for him and shouldn't restrict him in any way. The fennec foxes love jumping around, so you have to make sure that you have enough space for that. The last thing you want is to restrict your animal in a place that does not allow him free movement. Before you decide to buy the fennec fox, it will be great if you could assess how much space you have in your household that the fennec will be able to use.

5. Bringing home a healthy fennec fox

A major concern that many prospective owners and buyers of the fennec fox have is how to make sure that the animal that they are getting home is healthy. It is extremely critical that you get a healthy fennec fox to your home because once you get an unhealthy pup, you will only make things worse for yourself and the fennec fox. You will not know how to care for the sick pet. The pet's health will deteriorate. You will be spending thousands of dollars just on the health of the animal.

In the excitement of getting a new pet, you shouldn't forget the basic checks that you need to do before bringing the fennec fox home. The last thing that anyone would expect after finding a breeder and getting an animal is that it is not in good health. You should pre-check before you get the fennec fox to avoid introducing an unhealthy animal to your home.

The following pointers will help you to make sure that your future pet is in the prime of its health:

- First and foremost, you should check the health card of the fennec fox that you wish to buy. All good breeders will maintain a health card, which will have all the details of past injuries and infections. This health card will also help you to understand the vaccine cycle of the fennec fox. You will be able to understand which vaccines have been completed and which ones are due.

- It is generally believed that an animal's eyes are the index to his health. You should check the fennec's eyes. They should be bright and shiny. It is important that you find nothing abnormal with the eyes. In case you do, don't risk buying the animal or at least talk to the breeder.

- It is important that you closely examine your fennec. You should look for any abrasions on his skin. His skin should not be torn or bruised from anywhere. You should closely look for any kind of injuries. If you find anything that does not seem normal, then you need to discuss it with the breeder.

- The fennec should not have any broken limbs. You should be able to check this manually. You should look for any hanging limbs. A hanging head or limb could mean that the pet is severely injured. Carefully inspect the tail and stomach area also.

- You should make it a point to check the body temperature of the fennec fox. The body temperature should be normal. If you find it to be too high or too low, you should talk to the breeder about the probable reasons. The fennec fox could be suffering from some kind of infection.

- It is advisable to take the help of a qualified veterinarian to be sure of the pup's health conditions. He will be the best judge of his condition. The vet will also be able to guide you on how to take care of the health of the pup.

- Once the fennec is with the vet, you can be sure that he is in safe hands. You should discuss at length about the concerns that you have regarding the fennec fox. You should follow all the instructions that the doctor gives you because they will be for the benefit of the young animal. You should only keep the fennec fox if you are convinced that you will be able to care for the little animal.

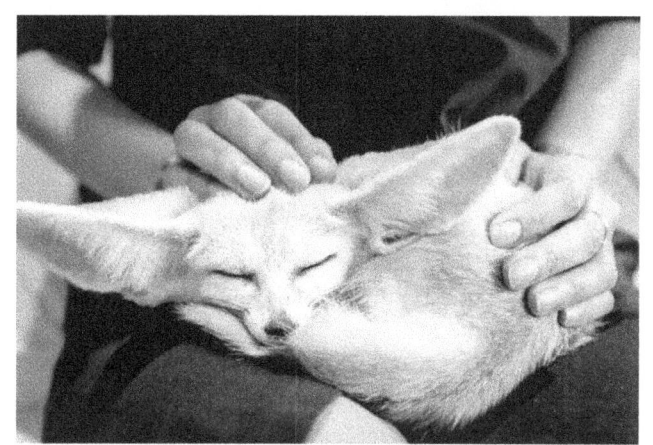

Chapter 2: Understanding the Animal in its Natural Habitat

If you are an owner of a fennec fox or if you wish to buy a fennec fox in the future then you should lay emphasis on learning about the natural environment of the fox. When you learn more about the natural environment of an animal, you understand him better. You will understand how the animal has adapted over time and how he communicates with its peers. You will also be able to relate to his natural behaviour. This will help you to be a better owner and will also help you to train your fox better.

The fennec fox is very small in appearance. This does not mean that the challenges that you face will also be small. It is not easy to domesticate a fox. They can be very difficult if not handled well. But, there is a reason to the way they are, and you should aim at understanding those reasons. For example, your pet might make a lot of noise at night. While you might choose to punish the fox for such behaviour, this behaviour will weaken your bond with your pet. You should understand the reasons behind these noises and try to look for alternatives. The noises that the fox makes at night time are for communication and also for defence. If you understand this natural behaviour of the fennec fox, it will be easier for you to deal with them.

The more time and effort you devote to your pet fox, the better it is for both you and your pet. The pet will also start loving you. This will give you immense satisfaction as a pet owner. So, to be a better owner, understand the foxes natural behaviour and his natural environment better.

As the owner of a new pet, it is important that you lay enough emphasis on understanding the habitat conditions of the pet animal. An animal should be kept in an environment that closely resembles his native habitat. For example, you can't expect an animal that dwells in a very cold environment to do well in humid temperatures.

The way an animal lives, eats, behaves and responds is highly dependent on his natural habitat. An animal found in the wild will be ferocious and his diet requirements will depend on what is available to him around his natural habitat. So, when you make an attempt to study the habitat of the fennec fox, you actually study the behaviour of the animal in depth. This will help you to domesticate the animal in a better way.

Every animal is so used to its own natural surroundings that as the owner of a new pet, you should make sure that you fulfil the habitat requirements of your pet animal. If you can't provide your pet a habitat that keeps him happy and safe, then you will fail as the owner of the pet. You need to make sure that the pet gets what would make it happy. But before you can do so for your pet, you should be able to understand what your pet needs. It is very important that you understand the habitat requirements of the animal.

1. Range, geographic location and climate

It is known that fennecs are most commonly found in dry areas. They are primarily found in the deserts of North Africa and also Asia. When it comes to deserts of North Africa, they are found in deserts of Egypt, Morocco, Sinai Peninsula, Kuwait and Niger.

Since the pet trade became very prevalent and easy, the range where the fennec foxes can be found has diversified. They are domesticated all over Europe and also the USA. Many zoos all over the world also keep these animals. They are kept there to preserve their species. These animals are also used for various research.

It is also important that you understand the kind of climate the fennec fox is subjected to. More than half of the locations where the fennecs are found receive little to no rainfall. It is known that the central part of the Sahara Desert will only get almost one inch of rain per year. This amount is too low to sustain life, but still many life forms have adapted to this extreme condition. Many other parts of the desert might get about four inches of rain in a year. But, another problem with the rain is that the rains are not regular throughout the year.

The average temperature of the Sahara Dessert is recorded somewhere around 30 degrees C. This is the average temperature recorded during the day time. This is just the average temperature. The hotter days have recorded temperatures close to 55 degrees C. This temperature is very difficult for any form of life. The air is humid and heavy, making life more difficult. The Sahara is known to have one of the most extreme temperatures in the world.

While the days are humid and extremely hot, there is a drastic temperature change during the night time. The air is mostly dry and there are no formations of clouds over the Sahara. When the sun sets in the evening, the temperature drops drastically and suddenly. The temperature falls and makes the nights just the opposite of the days. Compared to the hot and humid days, the nights are cold. While the day will be blazing at 30 degrees C, the night would be at a 2 degrees C. The temperature difference can go up to about 28 degrees C between the day and the night. When the winters approach, the condition becomes more challenging. The nights are not just cold, but freezing. There is snowfall, but due to the hot days, the snow will just vanish quickly. The point to be noted here is that the fennec fox has adapted to live in such extreme conditions. This will help you to understand the fur on its skin and paws and its nocturnal nature, among other things.

Topography

The Sahara is known to have sand dunes and sand seas, which are also known as shifting sand dunes. But, there are areas that have no sand. These areas support rocky terrain. The North of Sahara and the South of Sahara has some form of vegetation. The vegetation in these areas and the highlands is not very dense, but it is enough to sustain certain forms of life. It is known that the Central Sahara has little to no vegetation, owing to its weather conditions.

The Northern and the Southern areas support animals, such as fennec foxes, hyenas, rats and mice. The weather conditions can support vegetation that includes mainly shrubs and grasslands. A few tall trees and shrubs are also known to grow in these areas.

When it comes to water reserves, the river Nile is the only permanent source of water in the Sahara Desert. There are many other streams and places that have water, but they are seasonal and have a long dry spell.

The Sahara Desert will have rocky and hard terrains, and it will also have the sand dunes and sand seas. The most ideal place for a fennec fox would be where it can make a burrow. This makes sand dunes the perfect habitat for the animal. Stable sand dunes that have compacted soil make stable burrows. These are the perfect for a fennec fox. The fennec fox needs to build a burrow because that is the place where it will hide during dangerous times and during bad weather. His pup will also be raised in a burrow and food will also be hidden here.

The flora of the Desert

The most common vegetation of the Sahara Desert includes the shrubs, herbs, certain grasses and few trees. The less and unreliable rain, the humid environment and the excessive heat is responsible for this and can support only this kind of vegetation. The fennec fox can feed on this vegetation. These shrubs, herbs, grasses and trees help the fennec fox to get the required nutrition and water for its body.

Like most trees, the trees of the Sahara Desert are a source of food and also shelter to the animals in the desert. There are a few species of trees that can grow well in the extreme temperatures of the desert. Some of these trees are red acacia trees, fig trees, olive trees, date palms and doum palms.

2. Basic behaviour of wild fennecs

The fennec foxes are extremely energetic. They can run from one place to another in a matter of seconds. A new owner might find it very difficult to keep track of this pet due to his over enthusiastic and energetic nature.

The fennec fox also loves to dig in the ground. In fact, the fox will try to dig any and every place. The animal is used to digging in its natural environment. If the fennec fox is left on its own, the animal can dig a burrow of almost 25 feet in a single night.

In the wild, the fennec fox will dig a burrow and will remember the exact location even after months of digging it. The animal is not just fond of digging burrows, but it uses these burrows for various purposes. For example, if the fennec fox has some extra food, it will not throw the food away. It will save and store the food in the burrow. This helps the fox to feed himself when there is scarcity of food around.

The fennec fox is also used to running and jumping in its natural environment. They have these tactics to run from a dangerous predator or to catch a potential prey. In fact, a fennec fox can jump over four feet in a single time. They can reach a height of over two feet in a single jump. It is also known that the fennec fox is very sharp and agile. They might be running at a good speed, but if they sense danger they can change course in a matter of seconds. This can be done even in the middle of a run. They have great speed and stamina.

The fennec believes in being territorial. It can be observed that the animal uses the smell of his faeces and urine to mark his territory. These animals are very serious about their territories and boundaries. Once the fennec has established a territory, he takes it upon himself to guard the territory. He will display great enthusiasm and vigour in doing so.

The fox loves to be in groups because of its social nature. The fennec foxes can be spotted in groups of 10-12. In a group of fennecs, it can be observed that there will always be a leader. A male member will try to establish its authority by being the leader of the group. The leader will use his urine as a mark of the group's territory.

The fennec fox will like being in a group. But, it has been noticed that they don't like hunting in groups. The fennec foxes might be together all day, but when they have to hunt for food, they go all alone. They are nocturnal animals, which makes them more energetic in the night time. They usually venture out at night time to hunt for their food.

3. Communication with each other

It should be noted that only a limited number of studies have been done on the fennec fox in the wild. Most of the communication behaviour that has been noted has come from various owners' observations and experiences. It is well known that the fennec foxes are very noisy. Various studies have also suggested that these animals use different kinds of noises to communicate with each other. They make use of various kinds of sounds depending on the situation they are in.

There are some sounds recorded in the wild, which are made by male fennec foxes when they want to mate with a female. This type of sound is often called the mating sound. It is a deep and shrill sound. It is basically a signal to the females in the vicinity that the male fennec is looking for a partner. It should be noted that a male whose reproductive organ has been removed can't make such a sound.

They make barking sounds to indicate that they are in some sort of danger or that they are scared of something. It should be noted here that a pet fennec fox can also make such noises. But, if you care well for your pet, there is a very little chance that it will ever make a barking sound. If, by any chance, you observe your pet making such noises, stay away from them at such a time. They can get aggressive when they are scared.

Another very common sound that you will observe from your pet fennec is the purr sound. This is a sound when the fennec is a little irritated. The best thing to do when you hear such a sound is to give the pet some space. Don't go near him and let him calm down. If you have been holding your pet for too long in your arms, then this sound could be a signal to you that the pet wants to be a little free now. The purring sound can soon turn into a loud growl. This is when the fennec will want to bite whoever comes near him.

4. The social structure of the fennec fox

The social structure of the fennec fox will have the male fennec fox as the main head. This male will be the most dominant member of the herd. He would have a single mating partner. Their family will have the immediate litter of pups. Since the fennecs reproduce each year, their family would also include the previous litter if they survived. The fennecs like being in groups and families.

Another interesting fact about the social structure of the fennec fox is that even though other members in the group or skulk will be reproductively mature, not all of them can reproduce. Only the dominant male and his mating partner can mate each year. The reason behind this structure is cooperative breeding. Only one dominant pair breeds, while the rest of the members of the skulk cooperate in raising the pair's pups. The dominant pair has clear advantages in such a system. The other members protect their den, bring food and contribute in other ways to raise the litter.

The other members of the group get more time to hunt for the food. They also get to be a part of a larger group. The bigger the group is, the better it is for all the members because they all can be safer from predators as compared to smaller groups. So, under the social structure, all the members of the group gain in some way or the other.

Life span of the fennec fox

In its natural environment, it has been noted that the fennec fox will have an average life span of about 10-12 years. But, when these fennec foxes are held captive, they usually have a larger life span. The average in this case is about 12-14 years. The difference in the average life spans could be because of more favourable living conditions and constant food supply when the fennecs are domesticated. It should also be noted that that due to unfavourable environment and lack of food, sometimes the litter of pups are not able to survive for long.

5. Reproduction of the fennec foxes

According to all the studies done on the fennecs and the observations made by various owners, it is known that the fennec fox is a monogamous animal. Once the animal chooses its partner for mating, it will remain loyal to the partner for the rest of his or her life.

The fennec fox lays a lot of importance to family structure. The male and female fennecs will mate in the wild and the female will give birth to a young one with the purpose of forming a family herd. The female and male fennecs have separate responsibilities when it comes to raising the young ones, who are known as litters.

Sexual Maturity

It is known that the male fennec fox will reach reproductive maturity earlier as compared to the female fennec fox. After a male fennec is born, it reaches maturity at the age of 6-9 months. It can start mating at this time. On the other hand, the female fennec reaches reproductive maturity at the age of 6-11 months. Another point that should be noted here is that the fennec fox, male or female, will reach its full sexual potential only after it has attained the adult body size. Before that, the fox wouldn't be fully developed to reproduce.

The fennecs believe in only one partner. If a female fennec mates with a male fennec, it will mate only with that partner for her entire life. This holds true for a male fennec also. Once a female fennec gets pregnant and gives birth to a little one, both the male and the female do their specific jobs in taking care of the baby fennec. The male fennec will not enter the den of the family in the initial few weeks and will spend his time guarding and protecting the den and the baby from outside the den. This is important to keep the young one safe from potential predators. On the other hand, the female fennec will spend her time with the baby fennec, taking care of all its needs. The mother does not leave the baby at all for the first two weeks.

Till the baby fennec is six months of age, the father and the mother fox give all their time and energy to raising the baby. After six months, the fennec can take care of itself. In fact, he remains a part of the family pack and contributes in raising the next set of fennec babies or litters.

The litters are raised in safe burrows that the fennecs dig themselves. These burrows are like their territory. They are also referred to as dens. The fennecs are very smart when it comes to digging burrows for their families. They dig burrows under strong desert bushes. The roots of these plants give the burrow the much needed support. There are times when the fox makes multiple entries and exits to its burrow. In such a case, the burrow becomes a structure resembling a maze. This also helps the family of the fennecs to connect to other families or groups. These burrows are very deep. This also makes them safe from external dangers and harsh weather conditions.

Breeding

The breeding season is from the month of January to the month of February. After the mating, the gestation period for the mother fennec lasts for about 50-55 days. After this, the young ones or litter of kits are born in the month of March or April. The litter will usually have 2-5 pups or kits. The exact number is dependent on various conditions, such as food availability and weather conditions. It should be noted that an abundance of food is necessary for a larger number of fennec pups. The mother fennec will have a lactation period of 9-10 weeks. The weaning period of the pups is from 30-60 days after they are born.

Copulation

For the male and the female fennec fox, the copulation occurs during the second stage of the mating process. In the second stage, the genitals of the male and the female are inter-locked. This lock can remain for many minutes at a time. It can also last for hours together. The male fennec fox gets very concerned about his partner during the mating. The male will be careful and will look for potential dangers around so that they can't harm the female fennec in any way. The male fennec takes full responsibility to protect and secure the female during the entire process of mating.

Rearing of the kits or pups

The new born fennec fox is referred to as a pup or kit. The mother and father share responsibility to raise the new born pups. They are able to do so with the help and support of the other members in their group or skulk.

After the birth of the pups, the father and all the other male members of the group are supposed to stay outside the den. They can't come near the pups. The mother fennec gets very protective at this stage. She can even get aggressive when it comes to protecting her pups. She makes sure that no male member comes near the pups.

When a pup is born, it weighs around an ounce. The ears of the pup are bent and the eyes are closed and are almost sealed. The skin of the pup is of the colour grey. There are some pups that have dark marks on the grey coloured skin. These dark marks come on the fur of the fennec as they grow up. The fur of the newly born pup will be peach coloured.

The mother will nurse the kits under the burrow that was made by the other members of the family. This is the den of the group. While the mother takes care of the litter of pups, her food requirements are taken care of by the male fennec. The male fennec makes sure that the female has food during the gestation period and also the lactation period.

After about 12-14 days from the birth of the pups, they start opening their eyes. Around the same time, their ears that were earlier bent down start standing. They slowly start becoming erect. From this time, the ears of the pups will show many changes. There will be changes on a daily basis. This is the time when the ears are taking shape and form. It should be noted that within a few days from this particular time, the ears of the pups will be fully formed. While the body of the fennec fox will still be in the growing phase, the ears would have fully developed.

Slowly the kits will start development in other areas also. They will start playing inside the burrow or the den at about an age of four weeks. At this time, they will remain confined in the area of the den. Slowly, they will try to venture outside the den also. By the end of the fifth week, the pups would be playing near the exit of the burrow. Though they would not leave the area of the den, but they will start going around the peripheries of the den. This is the time when the father fennec will begin his interactions with the pups. Up until now, he was not allowed near the litter.

From the fifth week onward and till the tenth week, the pups will be showered with lots of love from all the members of the group and not just the mother and father. The members of the group will make sure that the kits are safe and sound. The mother and father will lick and carry the pups. The entire group will spend some great family time together.

When the pups are three months of age, they are allowed to go beyond the den. This is a crucial time in the life of the pup because this is also the weaning period. From the age of three months to the age of six months, the pups will start becoming independent fennec foxes. But, they will be closely watched by the mother fennec, father fennec and other members of the group. At about the age of 6-9 months, the pups gain full independence. The male fennecs will even start becoming sexually active during this time, though the females will have to wait for few more months to become fully sexually active.

6. Relationship with other animals

There are many studies that are being done to understand the relationship of fennec foxes with other animals in the wild. While it is known that the fennecs are cordial towards each other and like hanging out in groups, except for the times when they hunt for food, their relationship with other kinds of animals is not that great. They will kill and eat any animal that is smaller in size than them. And, they will save themselves from animals that are bigger in size. It is known that the fennec has a very good sense of hearing because it can hear things from far away. So, when they hear a potential danger, they just hide in their burrows.

7. Threats that they face

The fennec fox population across the world is facing many threats. While they have to battle it out with the bigger and more dangerous animals in the wild, there are other threats that they face. The human civilization is expanding in every possible direction. There have been many cases where the entire population of an area has diminished because of encroachment by the humans. For example, many parts of South Morocco that boasted of fennec foxes earlier have no fennecs left. They all vanished because of human beings.

Chapter 3: Things you Need to Know before Purchasing

If you wish to own a fennec fox, you can't just go and own one. There are many legal formalities that need to be fulfilled. But before anything else, you need to be sure that you are ready for the responsibility. A fennec fox is an exotic animal. This makes it a good choice for people who wish to domesticate rare animals. But, there is another side to this. Not many people would own a fennec fox, so you might not have observed one closely. Before you start domesticating the fox, there is not much experience that you carry. So, before you bring the exotic pet home, it should be your responsibility to gain as much knowledge as possible about the animals. You should understand the legalities, finances and responsibilities involved in domesticating a fennec fox.

It is important that you understand that you will face advantages as well as disadvantages once you decide to keep the fennec fox. This is true not just for the fennec fox, but for all animals. For example, a pet dog could be the best in giving you protection and safety, but the same animal could also turn out to extremely dangerous and ferocious towards the family members. A cat will be adorable and playful, but there are terrible mood swings that you will have to bear as the owner. Similarly, when you decide to keep a fennec fox, you have to understand the consequences of your decision. There will be some pros and also some cons related to the domestication of the animal.

This chapter will give you a list of things to ponder on before you buy a fennec fox. Various advantages and disadvantages of owning fennec foxes will also be discussed. This will help you to know whether you are ready for the responsibility or not. This is essential so that you make a well informed decision, and there is nothing to repent about later. If you are still contemplating whether you need the fennec fox or not, these pros and cons will help you to make a decision. Either the pros will motivate you to go ahead and get the animal home, or the cons will stop you from getting the animal home. Either way, you will be able to make a well informed decision and stick with it.

You should spend as much time as you want to make the decision because once you make the decision of buying a fennec, you shouldn't back out. If you buy a fennec and then suddenly decide that you don't want him, you will drastically affect the life of the fennec fox. A fennec fox is a very sensitive animal and your behaviour could change the way he looks at human beings forever. So, it is important that you understand every aspect related to the fennec fox in detail.

1. The legal aspect

It is extremely important that you go about the entire process of buying and domesticating a fennec fox the legal way. You should understand that we are talking about an exotic pet here, so the rules that bound it will be very different from the rules for other pet animals. You should make sure that you understand the related legal aspect before you go ahead and buy the animal.

The USDA governs the rules binding the domestication of exotic animals, such as fennec foxes. It is illegal to domesticate a fennec fox by capturing him from the wild. This is a punishable offence. Only certified fennec breeders can do so. As a prospective buyer, you will have to buy a fennec fox from a legally certified fennec breeder. It is illegal to buy a fennec fox without finishing all the legal formalities of your respective state. You should make sure that you understand the legal formalities for domestication of fennecs and fulfil them before you buy one. You should make sure that your state makes it legal to own a fennec fox because there are a few states that still don't allow the domestication of these exotic animals.

One of the major concerns of a first time owner of an exotic animal would be to understand the legalities involved in domesticating the animal. It should be noted that exotic animals come under a special category of animals, so it is imperative that the government of each state lays down some clear rules on the domestication of these animals.

If you reside in UK, then the rules that you need to abide by will be different from the rules of US. So, you should take out time to understand the specific rules of your particular state. In the United States, different states have different rules for the domestication of exotic animals. On the other hand, the United Kingdom has rules that are less stringent when compared to the rules of US. Many other countries in Europe also allow domestication of fennec foxes. There are rules and regulations for the same, but again they are not very stringent.

Legal formalities in USA

There are many states in the US that have absolutely no restrictions on keeping of these animals. For example, places like South Dakota, New York, Kansas and Utah allow the domestication of these exotic animals. On the other hand, there are many states that have completely banned the domestication of these animals. For example, the keeping of fennec foxes is not legal in Colorado, California, Mexico, New Hampshire, Oregon, Washington, Connecticut, Minnesota, Hawaii, Arizona, Georgia, Texas and New Jersey.

There are many states that allow the domestication of fennec foxes, but there is a rule to get the veterinarian approbation. The examples of such states are Montana and North Carolina. Some states such as Arkansas limit the number of fennec foxes you can keep. Some states have undergone changes in their laws. For example, states such as Maryland prohibit the domestication of fennec foxes now. But previously the domestication of the fennec fox was legal.

There are many states that allow the domestication of exotic animals, but they have regulations regarding their enclosures. You will be given clear instructions on how big the enclosure should be and how it should be constructed. Any error your part could get you into legal trouble. There are states that would want proof that the fennec fox was not hunted from the wild. In such cases, ask your breeder to provide you with a legal bill. You should also understand that the restrictions can be implied at any level in the government. For example, it is possible that the state does not impose any restrictions, but the city laws have specific rules. It is very important that you study the regulations regarding the fennec fox in your area very closely. You should not hesitate in contacting the wildlife division for answers to any questions that you might have. The laws and rules for such animals keep changing, so it is important to be updated on what's happening.

Legal formalities in UK

If you wish to own a fennec fox in the UK, then you should know that it is much easier to have one in the UK. As the prospective owner of a fennec fox, you will not be asked to have legal permits or licenses. The buying and domestication of fennec foxes is quite simple and easy in the UK and many parts of Europe also. It is important that you buy your fennec fox from a licensed breeder who has enough experience in this field. You might have to call the breeder even after you have bought the fennec home in case of any doubts or questions. The breeder should have enough experience to help you with your difficulties.

2. The right age of fennec fox to buy

Many prospective owners don't believe that the age should be a question when looking to bring a fennec fox home. But, age is a very important factor when you are planning to hand-raise a fennec fox. The earlier the fox comes to your home, the more time it has to get adjusted. This is better for the fox because he can adjust quickly. If you get a fennec fox that is not very young, then you have the additional pressure of breaking the fox's old habits. He will find it very difficult to adjust to the new surroundings and people. This will be very difficult not just for the fox, but also for you. The fox will be aggressive and restless and you just won't know what to do. So, always prefer buying a younger fennec fox.

Although it is advised to buy a very young fennec fox, it is also important that the fennec fox should at least be 4-6 weeks old. This will make sure that he was weaned from his mother and does not depend on his mother fox anymore. The pup that you buy should have been successfully weaned from drinking milk. This process will take time, so it is important that you don't buy a pup that is too young.

The problem with buying a kit before it is 4 weeks is that at such a young age, the requirements of the fennec fox will be very different. He would be very weak and would be on milk. As the new owner, you might find it very challenging to take care of the pet at this age. You will have to take the responsibility of bottle feeding the kit. There is every possible chance that you will be able to do it successfully and will be able to form a healthy bond between you and the fennec fox, but it is always better to trust the professionals for the same. A breeder is a professional and he has enough experience of hand-raising various pets. He would know exactly how the young fennec should be bottle fed. He would also be the best judge of when the fennec should be weaned from the bottled milk.

You should also make sure that the fennec that you wish to buy is bottle fed. It is important that the breeder has bottle fed the fennec fox from a very young age, preferably 2 weeks. A fox that is parent-raised instead of being bottle raised will be less sociable. Such a pet will not like the presence of humans and will have the tendency to get aggressive very quickly. You should make sure that you raise these questions when you meet the breeder. You should make sure that you know how the breeder has raised the fox. This will determine how well the fennec will adjust to your home and your family.

3. The right number of fennec foxes

You might be confused whether it is okay to domesticate more than one fennec fox at the same time. Legally, you will not be stopped from keeping more than one fennec, but there are a few other points that you need to consider.

There are only one or two states that exercise a law that limits you from owning too many fennec foxes at the same time. Apart from this, it is completely your prerogative to decide how many fennec foxes you would want to own. You should give time to understand the challenges that come with a fennec fox. This will help you to take a practical decision which will be good for you and also for your pet fennec fox.

If you have never domesticated a fennec fox before, then it is advised to buy only one fennec. It is believed that a pet fennec is quite similar to a pet dog and pet cat in his behaviour. In spite of all the similarities, there are a lot of differences also. So, just because you have domesticated cats and dogs before, you can domesticate 3-4 fennecs together.

A fennec fox can be very unpredictable at times. He might also get violent and aggressive. As a new owner, you will take some time to figure out how you need to deal with your fennec fox. Be ready to dedicate lots of time and love to your fennec. To be able to do justice to yourself and also the poor animal, it is advised that you bring only one fennec fox at a time. Once you understand how you should care for the fennec, you can buy another fennec fox.

A fennec fox is used to living in larger groups in its natural environment. So, a fennec fox will not mind another fennec fox in the vicinity. You will be surprised to see how well your pet fennecs will get along. You can buy more than one fennec without disrupting the growth pattern of each of them.

There are other reasons why you should contemplate bringing another fennec at home, when you already have one. It is important to understand whether you have the time and energy to spend on another fennec. Does it fit into your budget? This should be a major concern because buying and raising fennecs can be costly, so you should be sure before you decide to buy them.

4. Difficulty in rehoming

Once you buy a fennec fox, he can't be re-homed easily. This point is very important for all those people who are in a habit of buying animals and then selling them again to someone else. If you are not sure of a fennec, then don't bring one home. But, don't take a hasty and illogical decision.

By nature, a fennec is quite aggressive. When you make his life unstable, he gets all the more aggressive. You can't expect a pet to be in his senses if you keep changing his owners and home. A fennec fox will get attached to the one who spends time in raising him. This is the reason why it is advised to buy the fennec when he is young. He will form a special bond with that person. If the fennec has different owners at different times, it actually brings out the worst side of him. He won't trust anybody and will become very short tempered.

Fennecs are not natural pets, such as the dogs. Dogs will do their best to please their masters no matter what. On the other hand, the fennec will be friendly towards you only if it has formed a bond with you. If you fail to make that bond with the fennec, he will never be your true pet. He will be aloof of your presence and your authority as the master or the owner. Also, if the fennec is forced to change owners, he will stop treating owners like his masters. Fennec foxes are very sharp. They will judge you and act accordingly. A fennec fox can't be fooled into being a slave for his master. Your only chance to be his master is to form a bond with him by spending time with him and by being good to him.

You should make sure that you don't buy the fennec from another owner, even if he is offering you a much lower price. When you buy the pup or kit from the breeder, you can be sure that you are the first owner. This will allow you time and space to bond well with the new member of your family, your pet pup.

Another point that is worth being discussed here is that there can be some circumstances under which a fennec fox would have to be rehomed. It should be understood that the fennec could be under a trauma and it will take a great deal of effort to settle him down. It is advised that a new owner should not attempt something like this because the life of the fennec is at stake. An experienced person who understands the nature of fennecs and who is ready to give the extra love and care that the fennec might require should only attempt at rehoming the fennec fox. The fennec foxes in such cases will have to be treated like a small baby who needs a lot of love and attention and also good nutrition and care.

5. Advantages and disadvantages of domesticating Fennec foxes

Whenever you decide to domesticate an animal, there are always some advantages and disadvantages related to keeping the animal at home.

There are many people who are very impressed by the exotic and wild nature of the fennec fox. They think that this reason is enough to domesticate the animal. Such people don't understand the challenges that come with domestication of wild and exotic animals. There could be many other important points and issues that should be discussed before making the final decision for the animal.

A few advantages and disadvantages of domestication of fennec foxes have been discussed in this chapter. If you are a prospective buyer, then this section will help you to make a wise decision. If you have already bought a fennec fox, then this list of advantages and disadvantages will help you to prepare yourself for the challenges ahead. Once you understand the areas that would require extra work from your side, you will automatically give your very best in those areas.

Advantages of domesticating a fennec fox:

There are many pros of domesticating a fennec fox. This exotic animal can prove to be a great pet for your household if you raise him the right way. The various advantages of domesticating a fennec fox are as follows:

- Fennec foxes are very small in size. They look adorable to each and every person. The fennec at your house will be the talking point of each and every visitor of the house. These animals are exotic and desired, and human beings are naturally attracted towards such beings.

- The fennec fox is a very energetic animal. This animal can be really fun to be around. The pet will entertain you and your family with its unique character. Everybody in the house will love the pet fennec. This is because of its very unique nature. The fennec fox will be very energetic, playful and a happy kind of animal. They will play all the time, running from here to there in seconds. If there are kids in your home, then they will fall in love with this unique animal. But, the kids should not be left with the fennec alone. This is important to keep them and the fennec safe and sound.

- The fennec fox has the habit of licking himself and cleaning himself. This habit of the fennec makes him similar to a cat, which also licks and cleans. You will not have to worry too much about the hygiene of the pet fennec. Though he will clean himself, it is always advised to bathe the fox once in a while.

- Fennec fox has a thick cover of fur, but the good news is that they do not shed much fur. Animals that shed too much fur usually create a lot of mess in the house. The owner is always cleaning the fur off the carpets and sofas. You will not have to worry about any such thing when it comes to your fennec fox.

- If treated well, they can grow to be entertaining and lovable animals. You will be delighted to see how much your pet will adore you with the passage of time. The fennec foxes are capable of forming great emotional bonds with their masters. This may require a great deal of effort and also time from your side. So, if you work on forming a good emotional bond with your fennec fox right from the beginning, you will not be disappointed by your pet.

- There are many people who believe that fennecs can't be sociable. This is not true. Though the fennec might take some time to interact well with the humans, they can be social and friendly in their demeanour. A very important point to note here is that their demeanour will depend a lot on how they are raised. The preparation has to begin right from the start. You can't expect them to suddenly become friendly after years. If they are raised to be social, they will be very social. So as an owner and a master, it will be your responsibility to ensure that the fennec gets a very healthy, social and happy upbringing. This will help the fennec to grow up to be less aggressive and more affectionate.

- There are many people who are afraid that the fennec fox might smell a lot. Most of the animals of the fox family have a very strong body odour. But, the fennec fox does not have a body odour issue. The animal will only secrete a gland that will make him smell when he is frightened and alarmed. Apart from that, he will not stink or smell bad on usual occasions. This can be a great relief for many people because who wants a pet who smells all the time?

- Fennec foxes live in groups in the wild. This makes them tolerant towards other fennecs and animals in general. If you have more than one fennec, they will get along with one another. If you have other pets that are not too small in size, the fennec will be cordial towards them also. You will not have to worry whether the pets are getting along or not.

- One of your main concerns could be the diet of the pet fennec. Even if you love your pet dearly, you would want to avoid any hassles while feeding the pet. You might also not have the time to prepare special food all the time. In case you domesticate a fennec fox, then you will not have to worry too much about the diet. The diet of the fennec is similar to a pet dog or cat's diet. Also, there are many diet mixtures and pellets available commercially. These easily available food items ensure that the right nutrition is given to your pet.

- Fennec foxes can live up to 15-16 years in captivity. You can make a strong emotional bond with your pet and can enjoy the fruits of the bond for years to come.

Disadvantages of domesticating a fennec fox:

While you have studied the advantages of domesticating a fennec fox, it is also important to learn about the various disadvantages that come along with it. Everything that has merits will also have some demerits, and you should be prepared for this. The adorable and friendly animal has his own set of challenges when it comes to domesticating them. It is important to understand these disadvantages so that you can be better prepared for them. Following are the disadvantages of raising a fennec fox:

- The fennec foxes are hyperactive by nature. They can get agitated and worked up very easily. This behaviour could be difficult for a first time owner. These animals have a very unique temperament, and it would require patience from your side to understand this kind of temperament.

- The fennec can run from one place to another in a matter of seconds. A new owner might find it very difficult to keep track of this pet due to his over enthusiastic and energetic nature.

- The fennec fox also loves to dig in the ground. In fact, the fox will try to dig every where. If the fennec fox is left on its own, he might try to dig in your sofas, beds, etc.

- If the fennec gets a chance, it will escape. The fennecs are popularly called 'escape artists' because of their ability to escape. If the fennec escapes, you will never be able to find him because they are very fast. They have acquired this ability from years of running from predators.

- The cost that you will incur while buying and shipping a fennec fox is more when compared to other pets, such as the dog and the cat. The fennec fox will cost you a little more. If spending too much money is an issue with you, then you will have to think twice before purchasing the fennec fox.

- You should make sure that you understand how much the fennec fox will cost you. You should also understand the various other costs that you will encounter while raising your pet. The food that you serve them might be easily available, but the right brands might not be too cheap.

- It is very difficult to litter train a fennec. The fennec will just relieve himself whenever and wherever he wants to. You will get frequent surprises on your beautiful carpets and sofas.

- The fennec foxes are very noisy. These animals use different kinds of noises to communicate with each other. This can get very difficult for the members of the family. They are definitely not suitable for someone who is looking for a quiet and calm pet.

- The fennec fox is very independent. This characteristic makes very different from usual pets. The fox is aloof and moody. He will come to you when he wants. He will not be emotionally dependent on you in any way.

- These animals love playing and running around. These pets are fond of exploring things. You can pet them or hold them in your arms. But, they will not like to be held for too long. If you want a pet that will sit in your lap all day long or who will run around you, then the fennec fox is not for you.

- You should also understand that each fennec will be different from the other. While some might be too shy, others might love some form of human interaction. This is a process where you learn as you go. You always have to be a little ready for the unexpected. This is the only way to deal with a fennec fox.

6. Are you prepared to domesticate the animal?

You can't domesticate an animal only because the animal looks good. If this is the only reason that motivates you to bring an exotic animal home, then it is time that you rethink about your idea to domesticate the animal.

Fennec foxes are not very easy to keep. They require your patience, understanding, determination, time and money. If you don't have these things to offer to your fennec fox, then you will not be able to raise the pet well.

If you are contemplating on the idea of bring the fennec fox home, then it is important that you know whether you are ready or not.

- Do you have the time to take care of the pet? Do you have the patience that is required to domesticate a wild exotic animal?

- Do you meet all the legal requirements for domesticating the fennec fox? Is it even legal to domesticate them in your area? A fennec fox is not legal everywhere. You might also need a permit to take it from one state to another. You should make sure that you understand all the legal formalities before you buy the pet.

- Are you prepared for the long term commitment of raising the fennec fox? Do you have the means and the money for it?

- Fennec foxes are known to be very swift and fast. You will have to run around them many a time. Do you have that kind of energy to run around them?

- These animals will dig a lot. They will dig in the ground, on your floors and furniture. You need to be prepared for this.

- These animals can be very unpredictable. They can be very moody. Do you have the patience to deal with such behaviour?

- A small area is not enough for the overall development of the fennec fox. The fox needs enough space to roam around. Can you provide that kind of space in your home?

- Fennec foxes can be very noisy. They are known to make loud noises, sometimes in the night time also. If you wish to bring them home, you should be prepared for this.

- There are certain specific requirements that come along with each pet. For example, your fennec fox can't be kept in a cage for a very long duration. They have to roam around and exercise themselves. This makes it important for an adult to be around the fennec fox almost at all times. Can you make sure that such adult supervision can be provided at your home?

- Do you have a child under the age of 5 years at your home? Or are you planning to have a baby soon? If yes, then it might not be a good idea to buy the fennec fox. This is because kids under the age of 5 years should not be allowed near the fennec fox because of their unpredictable behaviour. Also, with a baby at home, you might not be able to give your pet the attention that it requires.

- If you are fond of pets that love to cuddle, then you should know that fennec foxes are not very fond of cuddling. If you take them in your arms to cuddle them, they will just play and enjoy themselves.

To ensure that your fennec fox lives a happy and healthy life at your home, it is more than important that you prepare yourself in the best possible way. You should make sure that you evaluate your resources well. It is also important to understand if your family is ready to domesticate the fennec fox or not. It might look like an overwhelming task, but it is important because bringing a new life home is a matter of great responsibility.

7. Things you should know before making a decision

Before you make up your mind to purchase a fennec fox, it is extremely important that you understand the nature of the animal. While the fennec fox can be very moody just like a pet cat, it can also be very playful as a pet dog. These animals have a very unique temperament, and it would require patience from your side to understand this kind of temperament. It is critical that you understand their nature well, so that you can take a final call on whether a fennec fox is suitable from your home or not.

There are many people who want to domesticate an exotic animal just for the sake of keeping such an animal at home. But, there is a lot that is at stake when you domesticate an animal. You have to make sure that the pet is suitable for your household. You should also make sure that you are suitable for the pet. The pet should be able to feel free and happy at your place. If you can't give a home to an animal, then you should rethink your decision to domesticate the animal.

Personality of Fennec fox

When you are looking at bringing a fennec fox home, it is extremely important that you know the personality of the animal. You can't domesticate an animal with some unreal expectations. You should know what you can expect and what you can't.

The fennec foxes are lovable and adorable. They are unique in many ways. You can't expect them to be your regular pets that will run around you all the time for everything. These animals need their space and time out. But, that does not mean that they are not fun. These animals will play with you and will make you fall in love with them, but you need to understand their unique temperament before you create any unreal expectations from them.

A fennec fox can be compared to a pet dog in many ways. The fox is playful and fun, just like the pet dog. The two animals possess large amounts of energy. In fact, a fennec fox can beat a dog when it comes to energy levels. The fennec foxes have too much energy in them. But, unlike a dog, a fennec fox will not crave your attention. A dog depends on his master for pretty much everything. But, a fennec fox is not like that. A dog tries all that he can to keep his master happy. You can't expect this behaviour from a fennec fox. The fox doesn't care about pleasing the master.

The fox is very independent. This characteristic makes them similar to cats. The fox is aloof and moody like the cat. He will come to you when he wants. He will not be emotionally dependent on you in any way. You should understand that your fennec fox will not hurt you if you pet him or try to touch him. But, they will not miss it if you don't do it. They don't crave for human contact, like many other pet animals.

These pets are fond of roaming around and exploring things. You can pet them or hold them in your arms. But, they will not like to be held for too long. You should be okay with this. These animals love playing and running around. If you want a pet that will sit in your lap all day long or who will run around you, then the fennec fox is not for you.

Noisy pets

This could come as a shock to you and many others, but fennec foxes are very noisy. They are definitely not suitable for someone who is looking for a quiet and calm pet. In their natural habitat, the fennec fox is said to be nocturnal. They save their energy to deal with the humid environment. They are active through the most part of the night. So, you can expect your pet fennec fox to make noises even in the night time.

The fennec foxes can make many kinds of noises. In the wild, they use different sounds to communicate different signals to other fennec foxes in the vicinity. They make a sound that resembles the sound made by birds. This is to communicate with their fellow foxes. When the fennec fox is agitated and angry, it will make a barking sound. They also have a peculiar sound that they like to make when they feel all alone. If you play with them at this time, they will feel very happy and will also make sounds of happiness. These animals can bark and can also purr. They bark when they are in a bad mood, but they purr when they are in a happy mood. So, you know that if the fennec fox is barking, you need to go and give him some attention.

One way to deal with this aspect of the fennec fox is to make sure that the cage of the animal is far away from where you sleep. This will ensure that you can have a good sleep even if the fox makes noises in the night. You should also make sure that the cage is kept in a place where other people also don't get disturbed. You should also make it a habit to play with your fennec fox just before his usual bed time. This will tire the fennec fox, and he might just go to sleep. This way both, the fennec fox and you can enjoy a good sleep.

Smell

There are many exotic pets that smell a lot. Such animals need to be given a bath regularly if you wish to domesticate them. But, the fennec fox does not fall into this category. They don't smell. They also don't like to take a bath. So, you only have to bathe your pet occasionally.

The fennec fox might not smell, but it has a unique ability to emit foul smell. The scent gland of the fox is found at the very tip of its tail. When this gland is secreted, the fox can smell really bad. It is difficult to stand near the animal during such a situation. The secretion of the scent gland is like the defence mechanism for the fennec fox. When the fox is scared or shocked, the gland is secreted and a very bad odour is released.

It should also be noted that the urine and the faeces of the fennec fox does smell a lot. You can get rid of this smell to an extent by making sure that hygiene levels are maintained at all times around the fox. You can also make use of various good quality cleaning products to get rid of this kind of smell. You should also make sure that the fox does not urinate on a carpet because it will be very difficult to get rid of the urine smell from the carpet. You might have to get rid of the carpet.

It is important to understand that a good diet also goes a long way in balancing the odour of the urine and the faeces. An unhealthy diet can lead to unbearable odour, whereas a good balanced diet can balance the odour. You should make sure that you feed high quality food that provides the fennec fox with all the nutrients that it needs for proper growth and maintenance.

Does the fennec fox shed its fur?

As a new owner, this could be one of your major concerns. It can be very difficult if a pet constantly keeps shedding fur. The fur of the fennec fox is very thick. The reason behind the thick fur is that the fox has evolved and adapted over the years to have a thick fur. This thick fur protects the animal in the wild against the hard weather conditions. The fennec fox is able to keep itself safe and warm because of the thick fur. They are able to conserve the heat of their body and the fur also helps for insulation against the cold environment.

Many people worry that the fennec fox might shed its fur constantly when kept in a comfortable home environment. But, the truth is that the fennec fox does not shed its fur regularly. The fox will only shed the fur when there are drastic weather changes. You can be prepared for this when the seasons change. Apart from the season changes, you will not notice much fur shedding from the fennec fox. You can buy a comfortable comb or brush to brush the fur on a regular basis.

Chapter 4: Purchasing the Fennec Fox

Over the years, the fennec fox has become a very popular choice for pet owners. This animal belongs to the exotic category of animals. This is another reason as to why people want to own a fennec fox. A fennec fox is adorable to look at and can be fun to have in the household.

The fennec fox is a popular choice for domestication in the United States and also most part of the United Kingdom. Even though you might be very excited by the prospect of owning an exotic animal, it is important that you buy the animal from a reliable and trustworthy breeder.

You should make sure that you understand how much the fennec fox will cost you. You should also understand the various other costs that you will encounter while raising your pet. This understanding will help you to take an informed decision.

One of the most important factors that make the fennec fox so popular is the exotic looks of the animal. The fennec is small in size and has large ears. It has a cute face that makes people fall in love with him. But, before you go and buy the fennec for his looks, it is important that you know that the cost of bringing up a fox is more than the cost you would have to encounter while raising an ordinary pet.

1. Costs encountered while raising a fennec fox

Before you are all set to buy the fennec fox and bring him home, it is also important that you work on all the costs that will go into raising the animal. This section will help you in understanding what you can expect in terms of costs when you are planning to bring a fennec fox home. It is better that you plan the costs that you will incur while raising the fennec fox. This planning will help you to avoid any kind of disappointment that you might face when there are some payments that need to be made. Being well prepared is the best way to go about things.

Once you have spent money on buying the fennec fox, you should get prepared to spend more money on raising your fennec fox. It is better if you plan these costs well in advance, so that you don't get in a fix at the later stage. You can expect to spend money on the shelter, healthcare and food of the animal. While there are certain costs that will remain fixed, you will also have to be prepared for unexpected costs once in a while. As the potential owner, you should understand that it is not possible to raise an animal without any money. And, there is no one-time payment to take care of the fennec. You have to be ready to bear various costs continuously over the years.

There are basically two kinds of costs that you will be looking to incur, which are as follows:

The initial or one-time costs: The initial costs are the costs that you will have to bear in the very beginning of the process of domestication of the animal. This will include the one-time payment that you will give to buy the animal. There are other costs that would come under this category. The initial costs that you will face when you are all ready to domesticate a fennec are the purchasing cost of the animal, the permits and the license cost, the vaccines, costs of food containers and the costs of the cage and enclosure.

The monthly or regular costs: Even when you are done with the one-time payments, there are some other costs that you won't be able to avoid. These costs can be planned well in advance. You can actually plan these regular costs long before you bring the pet home. You can also maintain a journal to keep track of these costs. The monthly costs are the costs that you will have to spend each month to raise the fennec fox. The costs will include the cost of the food requirements and health requirements of the fennec fox. The various regular veterinarian visits, the sudden veterinarian visits and replacement of things come under the monthly costs category.

Cost of buying the fennec fox

In comparison to other regular pets, the fennec fox costs you a little more. This is because it comes under the exotic animals category. The initial cost of purchasing a fennec fox will definitely be higher when compared with the initial cost incurred in purchasing other animals, such as cats and dogs. If money is an issue with you, then you will have to think twice before purchasing this exotic animal. On the other hand, if spending money is not an issue then you should understand the other important factors for raising a fennec fox and accordingly make a decision.

The fennec fox might look very small, but they are quite expensive. If you are looking to buy a small fennec (pup or kit), then you can expect to incur a cost of 1000 dollars to 3500 dollars. The average that you can expect is around 1500 dollars, but some breeders charge more money than others. The main reason for them being so expensive is that fennec foxes are not easily found. Your breeder might have to wait and face many difficulties before he can get one. This justifies their exotic nature and their high cost.

If you want to buy a fennec fox, then you should not waste time at regular pet shops. You will not get your fennec from there. There are special breeders who will be able to provide you with a fennec for a cost. Another important factor behind the high costs of the fennecs is that there are not many licensed breeders. There are limited breeders that deal with the breeding of fennec foxes. This makes it all the more difficult to get these foxes. Good breeders will always make sure that the fennecs that they possess are in the prime of their health. They will take care of their vaccines and health in general. This again means that the breeder will charge more. If your breeder has taken care of the vaccines and sanitisation of the fennec fox, then you should be fine with paying a little extra to this breeder because he has saved you from running here and there to get these important procedures done.

Cost of shelter

When you bring a pet home, you have to make the necessary arrangements to give it a comfortable home. The shelter of the animal will be his home, so it is important that you construct the shelter according to the animal's needs.

Fennec foxes are nocturnal animals, which makes them very active during the night time. If their shelter is not comfortable, the pet will be restless all the time. Even if you construct a very basic cage for the animal, it should have the necessary comfort. This is a one-time cost, so you should not try to save money at the cost of the pet's comfort.

The cost of shelter will depend on the size and the type of the shelter. You can expect to spend anywhere between 300 dollars to 500 dollars for the shelter of the fennec. You can get a basic yet comfortable cage for about 300 dollars. The cage will require some basic stuff, such as bedding and toys. These are the extra costs that you will have to incur in addition to the cost of the cage.

Cost of food

A domesticated fennec fox will mostly be fed cat and dog food. But, fennecs are omnivorous, so it is important that the fennecs are served more foods apart from the basic dog food and cat food. You might also have to include various supplements to give your pet overall nourishment. This is important because if the animal does not get all the appropriate nutrients in the right amount, his health will suffer, which again will be an extra cost for you. So, make sure that you provide all the necessary nutrients to your pet animal.

You should be prepared to spend about 50 dollars to 60 dollars on the diet of your pet fennec per month. The costs will vary depending on various factors, such as the brand of products that you choose and also your exact location. The kinds of food that you feed your pet will also affect the exact food cost that you encounter per month. You should remember that the more lax you are regarding the money that goes into food costs, the lesser would be the amount of money that would go into health care. If your pet is well fed, it will not fall sick that often. This will automatically reduce the amount of money that you would have to spend on the veterinarian costs and medicine.

Cost of health care

It is important to invest in the health of a pet animal. This is necessary because an unhealthy animal is the breeding ground of many bacteria and viruses. This means danger for the pet and also the members of the family.

The fennecs are exotic animals. You should understand that taking care of them will require special skills. You should make sure that the veterinarian that you consult for your pet fennec is experienced in handling such animals. You should also be prepared to spend more money on their health than what you would have spent on your pet cat or dog.

In the initial months, you will have to spend money on getting the vaccines for the fennec fox. These vaccines are critical to save the pet from diseases and deficiencies at a later stage, so make sure that you don't miss them. There are many breeders that take care of the vaccines of the fennec before giving it to the new owners. You should talk to your breeder regarding this. The breeder might include the money spent on vaccines in the final price that he might charge for the fennec fox. Either way, you will be spending some amount of money on the initial vaccines. You should also keep track of the vaccines, so that you don't miss any.

You will have to take the fennec to the veterinarian for regular visits on his health. He will be able to guide you regarding any vaccines that the pet may need. It is advised that for the very first year of domestication, you should keep about 300 dollars aside for health care of the fennec fox. You should also be prepared for unexpected costs, such as sudden illness or accident of the fennec fox. Health care is provided at different costs in different areas. So, the veterinarian in your area could be costlier than the veterinarian in the nearby town.

Cost of hygiene

A pet needs to be clean and hygienic. If you fail at maintaining hygiene levels for your pet, it will only lead to other complications. The entire household will be affected if the pet is not clean. Germs travel very fast, and before you realize there will be many hygiene related issues in your entire house. But, as the owner of the fennec, you don't have to worry much about the cost of hygiene for your fennec fox. You will only be required to spend a basic amount each month.

The fennec fox is not very good when it comes to litter training. But, there are many owners that insist on litter training. If you too wish to litter train your pet fennec, you will have to buy the required products. Your fox will not need a regular bath. This eliminates the need to spend too much money on bathing essentials. You should invest in a high quality cat shampoo. This will be enough for the occasional baths of the fennec fox.

You will also be required to invest in a good detergent. This will be needed to clean all the areas where the fennec fox might urinate. This again is a very basic cost that you will have to encounter. Apart from the detergent, you should invest in some good cleaning products and sanitizers. This will be necessary because the smell of the urine will be difficult to get rid of. You will need these cleaning products to eliminate the smell of faeces and urine of the fennec fox from the floor or from the cage area.

On an average, you can look at spending 15 dollars to 30 dollars on the hygiene requirements of your pet. This is an essential cost so that the surroundings of the fennec fox can be kept clean.

Other costs

Although the main costs that you will encounter while raising your pet fennec have already been discussed, there will be some extra costs that you will have to take care of. Most of these costs are one-time costs. You will have to spend money on buying pet beds, food bowls, blankets, a pet collar, hammock, pet carrier to carry the pet around and some toys for the pet. You can expect to spend some 200 dollars on these costs.

You should also regularly check the various items in the cage of the pet. If you think that something needs to be repaired or replaced, you should go ahead and do it.

2. Choosing the breeder

When you have made up your mind to bring a pet fennec fox home, you need to start planning the important costs that you will encounter. But, in the middle of all this, you should remember that should not just buy the pet from anywhere. You need to make sure that you buy the fennec from the right source. You should look for the best breeders in your area and should choose the very best among them.

In the US, the legal breeders of these fennec foxes have to be directed and regulated under USDA. You should check whether your breeder is regulated by the same. It can be an overwhelming task to choose the very best breeder. The following points will help you to choose the right breeder when buying the fennec:

- There is an official authority for animal control. If your breeder is not recognised by the authority, then it is illegal to buy an animal from him. Make sure that the breeder has an official license. You should not hesitate in asking the USDA number of the breeder. This is an official license number that the breeder should be possessing. The online USDA license search tool will let you know whether the license number is valid or not. It is important to be very sure about the breeder and his official capacity to sell before you go and buy an animal from him.

- A good breeder would have prepared a health chart of the animal for potential buyers. This health chart will let you know whether the vaccines of the animal are on time or not. The breeder should have ideally taken care of the vaccines of the fennec and should also inform you of the pending ones. You should talk to your breeder at length about the various vaccinations of the fennec fox. You should also understand whether the cost of the vaccines is included in the final price of the fennec fox.

- It is important that your fennec fox was in safe and experienced hands before you buy him. You should make sure that your breeder has considerable experience in handling fennec foxes. You should try to avoid first time breeders. An experienced breeder would have cared well for the fennec fox.

- You should never feel ashamed to ask questions from your breeder. Raising a fennec fox is a responsibility. To be able to perform your responsibility in the best possible way, you should be well prepared. You should ask all relevant questions from your breeder. It is important that your breeder has adequate knowledge regarding fennecs. If he has the right knowledge, he can impart the same to you.

- A good breeder will always ask you questions before giving you the fennec fox. The good breeder will want to make sure that you are ready for the responsibility of the new fennec. The breeder would be interested not just in money, but also assurance that the pet will be safe at your place.

- A pup that is raised by his own mother will not make an ideal pet. You need make sure that the pup that you intend to buy was hand raised by the breeder. This is important because such fennecs will learn to socialize from an extremely young age. This will make them friendlier and less aggressive towards human beings. The pup should have been separated from the mother fennec at least at the age of two weeks.

- Another point that should be one of your main interests is the parent fennecs of the fennec you wish to buy. It is important that the parents are not related to each other because if they are, then there is a great chance that the pup will have many health complications at a later age. You should discuss this point with your breeder.

- There is a chance that you won't be able to find a local breeder for a fennec fox. In such a case, you will have to ship in your fennec from a breeder. Make sure that the breeder is ready to ship the fox. Apart from paying for the shipment, you should also make sure that you have the required permit to ship the animal from an outside town. You can also look to buy a shipment insurance to cover for any mishap that might happen on the way. Make sure that shipping the fennec fox from somewhere outside is the last option that you exercise. If you can find a good local breeder, then there is nothing like it. You can see your fennec before buying him. You can visit him multiple times and can talk to the breeder at length before you are required to take a final decision.

- If you are shipping the fennec fox, then don't forget to look at the pictures of the fennec fox before you finalize the deal. This is the least you can do to be sure.

- If you wish to buy a fennec fox, you will not get one the next day or even in the next month. There can be a long waiting list before your chance to buy the animal comes. You should be patient and should be mentally prepared for such an event.

- It goes without saying that you should make the payment to the breeder only by legal and authorized channels. This is important so that you aren't duped by a fraudster pretending to be a breeder.

- A good breeder will always give you a sample of food that he was feeding the fennec. This is because if you suddenly wean the fennec away from the food, he might get sick. You should keep feeding him the same dry foods for some time. You can slowly introduce new foods to him and make him leave the original dry foods.

- You should make sure that the fennec fox that the breeder is offering you is in the prime of its health. You should never commit the mistake of bringing a sick fennec fox to your home. Check the health card and even consult a veterinarian if required before making the final deal.

- To save yourself and your family from falling prey to any scam, it is important that you do your homework well. Before finalising on a breeder, gather as much information as possible about him. Talk to people who might know him. These are some simple steps to make sure that you are not being duped.

- You should also understand that a legal transaction with a legitimate breeder could cost you few more dollars. But, this should be fine with you. Hand raising fennec foxes is not an easy task, so not all breeders in your area will do it. There are not many pups available throughout the year and it is difficult to hand raise them after weaning them from the mother. It is critical that you buy your fennec pet only from a certified license holding breeder.

Finding a breeder

In this age and technology, everything has become easier, even finding a fennec fox. Though it can be a difficult task to locate a local fennec fox breeder, there are many breeders that have started advertising their services online. There is a lot of information on the Internet. If you stay in the United States of America, then it is not that difficult to find a good breeder. It is believed that though domestication of fennec foxes has started becoming quite normal in the United Kingdom also, it is still not that easy to find a breeder there.

As a potential owner, it is completely your prerogative to look for the best breeder that you can possibly get. The following sites will help you in your endeavour to locate a breeder near you, but remember these sites are not being endorsed or advertised here, and it remains the potential owner's responsibility to authenticate the breeder's claims:

In USA:

1. www.fennecfoxes.net: If you are residing in USA, then this site can be of real help to you. The website has a comprehensive list of many breeders in the United States of America. This list will help you to give your search for the right breeder a direction. The list of various breeders is provided under the heading 'breeder directory'. You can look for the various breeders and narrow down your search by finding out the ones that are in your area. You should always give preference to a good breeder than to someone who is nearby. It is always advisable to spend extra dollars to get a fennec from far away than compromise on the quality of the fennec fox.

2. Flashmanfoxes.com: This is the website of a very popular breeder in US. This breeder is a knowledgeable breeder who is considered very trustworthy by his clients. He knows a lot about the foxes, which makes him a good breeder to deal with. You can clear all your doubts about your pet before you bring him home.

3. CreaturesGreatnsmall.com: This is again a very popular breeder website in Indiana. The breeder is popular among potential owners of fennec foxes because the owner is ready to ship to various areas. This can be a great help for someone who is unable to find a decent breeder in his or her area. So, if you like the fennec fox that this particular breeder has to offer to you, you can rest assured that the fennec fox will reach you. The breeder will make the necessary arrangements. It is important to check the areas where the breeder is ready to ship. You should also make sure that the extra cost of shipping fits into your budget.

4. You can always Google for various breeders in your area. There are many popular fennec forums that you can become a part of. This will keep you in touch about the latest popular breeders. It is also important that you acknowledge the time that any breeder spends with you. It is always better to acquaint yourself with enough knowledge before contacting the breeder. If you are not serious about owning a fennec fox, what is the fun in contacting various

breeders? Keep things clear at your side and then go on to locate breeders for fennec foxes.

3. Caring for the fennec fox

When you bring a pet home, it becomes your responsibility to raise the pet in the best way possible. You have to provide physically, mentally, emotionally and financially for the pet. Before you embark on this journey of raising your pet, it is important to evaluate your resources and make sure that you are ready for the pet.

You should know that the requirements of your pet fennec fox will be very different from the requirements of your pet cat or dog. You can't expect to face similar challenges when domesticating two entirely different pets. Preparation is the key to success, so it is all the more important to prepare the domestication of your fennec fox well.

The chapter will look into the various concerns that you might have when looking at getting the fennec fox home. This chapter is an attempt to list all the general and important reference points for understanding the fennec foxes in a better light. These points can be a quick guide when you are looking for some specific information about fennecs.

Understanding the requirements of the pet animal

It is important to have a reference guide for understanding the requirements of the fennec fox. This will help you know your pet better. Domesticating a fennec fox as a pet can be a very pleasant experience if you are prepared with what you can expect from the experience. The more you know about your pet, the easier it is for you to understand him. You will be able to prepare yourself and equip yourself better. There are many responsibilities that come along with the pet animal to your home. You need to be ready for them. For some people, this experience can turn into a nightmare if they are not prepared and well equipped.

Bathing requirements

When the fennec fox is in its natural environment, it cleans itself with the help of its saliva. The animal licks himself and keeps himself clean. This means that this animal does not require regular baths. You can bathe your fennec fox only occasionally or when they get dirty because of getting into mud or sand.

It is important that the fox is comfortable with the idea of bathing. For this, you should give the fennec fox regular baths when it very young. You can easily use mild shampoos or cat shampoos for your fennec fox. You can also consult the veterinarian in case you have any doubts.

If your pet is infested with fleas, then a bath can help to get rid of the fleas. You can use an anti-flea shampoo for the pet. You should also know that the foxes are afraid of running water. So, when you decide to give your fennec fox a bath, make sure that the water is collected in a tub. Make sure that the water is lukewarm. The fennec fox will not enjoy bathing. So, try to keep the bathing time as short as possible.

Right containers for the food and water

While you will spend a lot of time and energy in deciding the right menu for the fennec fox, it is also extremely important that you pay importance to the containers. These containers will be used to serve water and food to the pet fennec. While you might wonder the importance of food containers, you should understand that dirty containers are carriers of allergies and diseases. These allergies and diseases can further turn into serious problems if not treated well. So, it is important that you take care from the very beginning and make sure that the right containers are chosen to serve the food items.

You can consider the following points to make sure that the food is fed in the right way and in the right containers:

- The containers you use are safe for the animal. You should make sure that they are made from safe material. They should also be easy to handle for you.

- A poor quality container will make the food spoil. The spoilt food is injurious to the health of your fennec fox.

- The containers should also allow the pet animal to feed himself without any difficulty.

- The food and water containers should be sturdy enough to hold all the food and water.

- The water container that you choose should allow you to store good quantities of water for a long time. They should not break under the weight.

- It is very important that the containers are kept clean. The containers should be washed with good quality soap powder at least two to three times a week. You should also make sure that you remove the left-over food or dirty water from the food and water containers.

Neutering or Spaying

As a new owner or potential owner of the fennec fox, you might also be interested to know that many owners decide to neuter or spay their fennec foxes. Neutering is the term used to describe the act of removal of the reproductive organ of a male fennec fox. Spaying is the term used to describe the same action in the female fennec fox.

The reason why owners choose to do this is because the fennec fox, especially the male fennec fox, can get very aggressive once it reaches an age of sexual maturity. This aggression can be very difficult to control for the owner. The male fennec foxes also get extremely agitated when they come in close proximity of other male fennec foxes.

If you are contemplating the advantages and the disadvantages of neutering or spaying, then you should understand that there are many sides to neutering. The choice of getting it done should completely depend on how you want your fennec fox to be. It is important that you understand all the advantages and disadvantages of the process well so that you can decide whether you want the procedure done for your fennec fox or not. Even if you decide to go for it, it extremely important that you get it done from a good veterinarian. You should discuss your pet's heath and all other issues with him clearly. You should go for it only after you are 100 per cent convinced that your pet needs it.

The following are the few advantages of spaying or neutering fennec fox:

- If you decide to spay your female fennec fox, then you can save yourself from unnecessary pregnancies of the animal. A point that needs to be kept in mind here is that owners who are looking to breed the fennec foxes should avoid the process of spaying. The female fennec fox will lose its ability to get pregnant after spaying.

- The aggression in male fennec foxes can be a matter of great concern for the owners. It has been noticed that the male fennec foxes without their reproductive organs are much more loving and affectionate towards their masters.

- The male hormones are found in the reproductive organ. After the organ is removed, the animal faces a loss of the male hormones. This makes the male fennec fox calm. He loses much of his aggressive nature. This makes the animal more suitable as a pet for a family.

- Another advantage of this process is that after neutering or spaying, the fennec fox will lose some power of body smell. This can be a relief for you as the animal will be much more hygienic after this.

Chapter 5: Diet Requirements

By nature, the fennec fox is omnivorous. The animal can eat both plants and animal based food. It is important that the food that you give to your pet gives it proper nourishment. The fennec fox requires a diet that is high in taurine. Many fennec fox owners feed their foxes with canned cat food or dog food. It is important to give other food with the canned foods. You can also look to give them pills to supplement the nutrients that the food is not providing them.

The fennec fox should be given cat food once or twice a day. The food should be good quality. This canned cat food should be wet and it will form as a base to its food requirements.

1. Everyday diet for the fennec fox

As the owner or prospective owner of the pet fennec fox, it would be your foremost concern to provide proper nutrition to your pet. You should be looking at maintaining good health of your pet. The food that you feed your pet with could be lacking in certain nutrients. In the wild, fennec foxes feed themselves on plant based and animal based food. Many a times, the food given to captive fennecs is not able to provide the fennec with all the necessary nutrients. These pets are given commercial pellets. These pellets are known to compensate the nutritional deficiency that the animal might have due to malnutrition or insufficient food. You should also aim at providing wholesome nutrition to your pet fennec fox. To do so, you might also have to give him certain supplements. Supplements will help you to make up for these essential nutrients. You should definitely consult a veterinarian before you give your fennec fox any kind of supplements.

If you are looking at a guide as to what needs to be fed to your fennec fox on a daily basis, then the following points will help you a lot:

- Wet cat food should form the base of your diet plan. You should serve it to your fennec at least once a day. You can also serve it two times a day. Please make sure that this food is of premium quality. Since this is the chief food for your fennec, you should not compromise on the quality of the food because the health of the fennec should not suffer.

- You can put dry dog food in a basin and leave it near the fennec fox. The fennec fox can eat it when it is hungry. Again, it is important that the food is of a very good quality. The dog food has to be dry.

- You should also serve vegetables as a part of the daily diet of the fennec fox. This will give the required nutrients to the fox. You should make sure that you don't serve canned vegetables to the animal. The vegetables should be fresh and should be chopped nicely. If you don't have the time to chop vegetables every day, then you thaw, chop and freeze the vegetables. You can mix these pieces with the wet cat food. This will ensure wholesome nutrition to the fennec food.

- Since your fennec is an omnivore, you can feed some insects to it. This can be given any time during the day. You can feed the fennec with mealworm and crickets.

- You should make sure the fennec is given good amounts of taurine in the diet.

2. Snacks for the fennec fox

While there are certain food items that you should feed your fennec every day, you should also plan for some snack items. You can feed these snack items once in a while to change the regular taste of the fennec's food. You can also use these snack items as small meals in between meals. You would also have to look into snack options along with the regular everyday meals for your fennec fox. The following food items can be served as snacks or treats:

- Chicken can be served to the fox along with the regular wet cat food. You can also serve the chicken as a stand-alone dish. Make sure that the chicken is well cooked. The fennec is used to eating animal meat in the wild, so it will easily digest the meat. You should make sure that you introduce only those meats to him that can be served later also.

- Eggs can also be given to the fennec fox. You can boil the eggs or scramble the eggs. The fennec will enjoy this treat for sure.

- You can also serve fresh fruit slices as treats for the fox. But, it should be remembered that large quantities of fruits is not healthy for the fox as they can cause a problem of diarrhoea. You should only serve them sometimes, after carefully removing the seeds of the

- fruits. The fruits that you can make use of are bananas, apples, melons, blueberries and strawberries.

- Another option for a snack item is pinkie mice. Your fox will love this treat. They are easy to digest for the animal.

- Dates and figs can also be served to the fox occasionally. You will have to note the reactions that your pet gives this particular treat. If he does not seem to enjoy them, then you can discontinue the dates and figs.

- You can also serve dog treats that are easily available on the market to your fennec fox. The fennec will surely enjoy these dog treats. You can keep them as the main snack items along with chicken.

- You can also look for packaged dry cereal. It is healthy and is easily available. This can be a good snack option if the fennec grows to like the taste of this treat.

It is important to note here that you don't have to feed all these snack items every day. These food items are varied options that you can choose from. Also, you should make sure that you don't over feed the fennec. This will make him sick. He only needs to be given the right amount of food.

3. How much food to serve?

As the owner of the new pet, you might want to give all the love and food that you can to your pet. But, giving too much food is not healthy. You should limit the quantity of food that you serve to the pet.

There are many snacks you can choose from, but make sure that you don't serve all the snacks on a single day. Too many snacks in a day are not healthy. A snack is optional and is only a mid-meal option that you have.

The cat food or the dog food will be your base food for the pet. You should make sure that the food is of premium quality. Don't forget to check the main ingredients before you buy the food. Meat and taurine should be the chief ingredients of the packaged food. The food should be grain free. The dog food that you decide to buy should be suitable for puppies. If it is suitable for them, then it is suitable for your fennec fox.

There are many premium dry dog foods available, such as 'Wellness Core', 'Royal canine Chihuahua puppy 30' and 'Science diet for the small canines'. There are many premium wet canned cat foods available, such as 'Fancy feast of turkey or chicken', 'Prime fillets' and 'Nine lives veal and gravy'.

There are some important guidelines that you should be following when you are feeding your fennec fox. They are as follows:

- Your fennec fox will not like to be disturbed while he is eating his food. Let the fox enjoy its food. Give him the space and the time.

- You should make sure that the fennec fox is not served food with any other pet. If you do so, then your fox will try to eat his own food and also the food of the other pet. To avoid such a situation, feed the two pets far away from each other.

- You should always remember that feeding only cat food or dog food is not a very healthy option. You will have to supplement the other nutrients that the fennec fox needs for his growth.

- There are many fennec fox owners that believe that serving raw foods is the best way to feed the fox. This allows the fox to be as close to its natural environment. But, there are many veterinarians that believe that this diet is not suitable for domesticated foxes. If you take a decision of serving raw stuff to your fox, then it is important that you understand the advantages and the disadvantages of such a diet. You should talk to your vet at length to understand this diet well.

Amount of taurine in the pet's diet

It is important that the everyday diet of the fennec fox is able provide it with all the necessary nutrients. The fennec fox needs good amounts of taurine in its diet. The deficiency of taurine can lead to many diseases in the fennec fox. So, it is important that the food items that are served to the fox are rich in taurine.

As a new owner, you might also be perplexed as to how much is the right amount? You might not know how to maintain the right quantity of taurine. What if you there is an over dose? What if the quantity is not enough?

To begin with, you should keep a track of what you are feeding your fennec fox throughout the day. Keep a check on all the vegetables and meat items that you are serving to the fennec. Raw food is a great source of taurine. If you are following a raw food diet, then the taurine requirements for the fennec would be fulfilled. But, a raw food diet would lead to deficiency of some critical nutrients for the fennec fox. You should make sure that you supplement these nutrients. There is also a possibility that your fennec fox will not enjoy the raw food diet. He might want foods with other flavours and tastes.

If you are feeding your fennec fox with only commercial food, such as store bought cat food and dog food, then you will have to supplement taurine in some other way. These commercial food items are not too high in taurine. If you keep feeding your pet only the dog food and cat food, you will soon realize that the fennec is deficient in certain nutrients, such as taurine. This could lead to some serious infections.

You would not have to worry about your pet suffering from an overdose. The pet fennec will not have to suffer from excess of taurine in his body. The body utilizes the amount of taurine that it needs, and the rest is simply excreted. If the digestive or excretory system of the fennec is not in place, then excess of taurine could be an added problem and complication. Otherwise, the excess would be come out in the faeces of the animal.

You can feed the fennec with food items, keeping in mind the taurine content. You could alternate the raw food with the commercial foods. But, if you still think that you are unable to fulfil the daily nutrient requirement of the fennec fox, then you can give him taurine tablets. You can easily find these taurine tablets. You can even order them online. If you are looking for taurine tablets, then 'PetAgtaurine' pills could be a good choice for you and your pet fennec. With the commercial food diet, you should give your fennec fox at least 1 one tablet in a day. You can also give 2 tablets to the fennec fox. If you think that the diet of the fennec fox is not enough to fulfil its taurine requirements, then you can look at giving it 2 tablets in a day.

The fennec fox might just swallow the tablet as a whole. But, if you feel that your pet is not taking the tablets that easily then you can crush and pound the tablet and mix it with the regular food of the fennec fox. This is an easy way of ensuring that the fennec fox is getting its daily dose of taurine. You can also get taurine in powdered form from a store near. You can easily mix this powder in every meal of the fennec fox. You should make sure that the taurine powder is pure and there is no adulteration. To be on the safer side, look for only premium and popular brands. You can look for a good quality taurine powder online also.

4. Foods that need to be avoided

You will have to be very careful when you are planning the diet for your fennec fox. A good diet will help to keep the fennec fox healthy and will also protect him from various diseases. There are many food types that are not suitable for your fennec fox. You can't randomly give anything to the fox because there are many foods that are dangerous for the fox. As a simple rule, you should always remember that all the foods unsuitable for a pet cat or dog are unsuitable for the fennec fox.

First and foremost, you should always keep the surroundings of the fennec fox clean and tidy. Your fox will try to eat anything and everything around it. You might find your pet eating the sofa covers or the little toys. You should make sure that small toys and other toxic items are not kept around the fox. The pet might choke himself in an attempt to eat the stuff.

You should always avoid serving foods rich in acidic content to the fox. Such foods are known to cause ulcers in the fox's stomach. You should also avoid giving anything spicy to the fennec fox. Keep the food simple and healthy. If you are giving meat, then you should make sure that it should not have bones because the bones can get stuck in the throat of the fennec fox.

If you are looking for a comprehensive list of food items that are unhealthy for the fennec fox, then the given list will help you. You should try to avoid these food items:

- **Caffeine**: You should keep tea and coffee away from your beloved pet. Caffeine can cause tremors, nausea, diarrhoea and coma in a fox. Sometimes, the children of the house can force the fennec to consume such food items just for some fun. So, it is important that you keep a check on what the kids are doing with the fennec fox.

- **Chocolates and cocoa beans**: These items are unhealthy for foxes, especially for the younger ones. These items can cause extreme restlessness in the pet and can also lead to complications. You should make sure that you keep these food items away from the fennec fox.

- **Salmon**: Raw salmon has a parasite that is extremely toxic for the fennec fox. You should avoid raw salmon at any cost. It has been noted that almost all cases of fennec foxes consuming salmon have died. Your pet wouldn't know that this food is not good for him. You should take it upon yourself to keep such foods away from the pet.

- **Raisins and grapes**: Though it is suggested that some fruits should be given to the fennec fox on a regular basis, grapes are not good for the fennec. Grapes and raisins affect the kidneys of the fennecs. If these food items are given for a longer duration, substantial damage is done to the kidneys.

- **Walnuts**: Another food item that is dangerous for the fennec fox are walnuts. You might believe that walnuts are healthy foods, so they should be fine for your fennec also. But, this is not true. The digestive system of the fennec fox is not able to digest the walnuts. If a fennec consumes them, he will experience vomiting and body weakness. In some extreme cases, the pet might also suffer from tremors.

- **Certain vegetables:** such as tomatoes, eggplants and bell peppers need to be avoided.

- **Avocado:** Another food item that is dangerous for the fennec fox is the avocado. The digestive system of the fennec fox is not suited to digest this food item. The fennec will experience diarrhoea and vomiting after it consumes this food. The fennec might also experience difficulty in breathing because of this food item.

- **Xylitol:** This is a very harmful compound for the fennec foxes. It will directly affect the liver of the animal. It is important that you know which food items contain this compound. Xylitol is found in chewing gums, sweets and toothpastes. You should make sure that you keep away these items from the fennec fox.

- **Macadamia nuts:** Another food item that is dangerous for the fennec fox are Macadamia nuts. The digestive system of the fennec fox is not suited to digest them. Macadamia nuts can cause vomiting and body weakness in the pet fennec. In some extreme cases, the pet might also suffer from tremors.

Chapter 6: Training the Fennec Fox

It is imperative to train a pet. This is a simple way to monitor their behaviour and to teach them what behaviour is acceptable and what isn't. There are many people who adopt the same training skills to train both dogs and fennec foxes. The reason behind doing so is that dogs and foxes are very similar in their behaviour. Though this could be true to some extent, fennec foxes are much more challenging than dogs. This makes the training of fennec foxes a little more complex and advanced when compared to training other pets.

A fennec fox is very curious and playful in nature. The curiosity of the fox makes him stubborn and difficult to teach. The animal is very intelligent, but can be very moody at times. While you can pet and praise a dog and make him do things, this technique fails on the fennec fox.

1. Is it possible to train a fennec fox?

Many of you might be wondering whether a fennec fox can actually be trained if he is so mischievous and stubborn. The truth is that they can be trained but you will be required to put in more time and efforts to do so.

You should understand the importance of training a fennec fox. The fennec fox needs to be taught certain things so that it does not get back to his basic wild behaviour. Apart from teaching him the right behaviour, training will also help to form a bond between you and your pet. It will bring the two of you closer to each other.

You should not make the mistake of starting the training of the fox when he grows up. The sooner you start the training, the better. You should start the training when the fox is very young. This will give the pet some time to learn and understand what is expected out of him. It is also important that the training is not stopped at any stage. The fennec fox will forget all the training and go back to his old ways.

A fennec fox is not extremely loyal towards its master. The animal has no desire to please the master or to keep him happy. This system won't work. You should reward him with something that he likes, such as a dog treat.

Your fennec fox can be trained for many things, such as bath training, harness training and public spaces training. If you wish to see your fox sit down when you ask him to or run to fetch a ball, then you will have to spend a lot of time training him because such skills don't come naturally to him.

When you are training a fox, you need to be aware of his basic nature. In the wild, foxes communicate by giving each other small bites. These bites are not fatal as they don't penetrate the skin. But, this behaviour can come as something very shocking for human beings. You must understand that biting is in the nature of the fennec fox. It will try to bite you at multiple occasions.

When you are training your pet animal, you need to teach him that biting is not okay. This might be difficult for you in the beginning. Don't play with your fox with your hands too close to his mouth; otherwise he will try to bite them. You should never encourage biting by rewarding him anything after the bite. Don't give the pet his treat for some time if he has bitten you because this will teach him that it is not okay to bite others.

If your pet comes in a mode where he tries to bite you continuously then you should give a small toy to the pet. Let him bite the toy. You should repeat this action whenever he tries to bite you. This will send a signal to the pet animal that it is not okay for him to bite you. It is important to send the right signals to the pet.

The most important point that you need to remember when you are training your pet is that it is not possible to train the fennec fox in just a few steps. The fox will forget and go back to his basic habits if you are not consistent. You will have to do the same steps again and again. These repetitive actions will require patience and time. It may take weeks or months before you see any positive results. If you don't see instant results, don't get angry, and don't hit the animal.

Pets are like small children. You have to deal with them with patience and love. If you beat your fennec fox out of frustration, you will rupture the bond between the two of you. He will detest coming to you and things will only get worse. If you think that punishing the pet will help to train him, then you should understand that the pet might not even realize which actions are leading to the punishment. It will only confuse him further. The skin of a fennec fox can break very easily. When you hit him, there is a great chance that he will be physically hurt. You should NEVER do so.

When you are training the pet, try not to chase him. Fennec foxes generally associate chasing with being held captive. If you wish to play with them, kneel on the floor. You should be on the same level as the fennec fox if you wish him to enjoy playing with you. You can also take the animal in your arms, but you need to know that they are not very cuddly. They will play in your arms for some time and then will want to come down. You should be prepared for such behaviour from your pet.

2. Harness training

Fennec foxes are really fast, so it can be very difficult for you to keep track of them. Many owners find it important to leash train or harness train the fennec fox so that it does not run away, especially when it is taken outside. There are times when you would have to take the fennec fox outside. If for nothing else, you would have to take the fennec to the veterinarian. Harness training can help keep some control over the animal. But, an important point that needs to be understood here is that even with the leash on, the fennec fox is so strong that it might pull the harness away and run. You need to be careful about this. You should make sure that you use a good quality leash and harness that allows you maximum control of your hands. You should always remember that once the fennec runs away, it is not coming back. The animal would just run away and would never return. Another option that you have instead of the harness is the usage of a travel crate. These crates are easily available. You can use a cat travel crate whenever you have to take your fennec outside. This will ensure that he can't run away anywhere.

3. Litter or potty training

There are many exotic animals that have a problem of body odour. These animals smell bad. A fennec fox does not have such a problem. But, the fennec has another problem. It is very difficult to potty train this animal. A fennec fox has he tendency to defecate wherever and whenever he wants to. He does not look for a safe spot. He does not stop the work he is doing. If you don't pay attention, the animal could even do this in your entire home. The breeder will take no responsibility, and you should be solely responsible for litter training the fennec. Even if you decide to take upon this challenge, you should know that you can never litter train a fennec fox completely. You might be successful to an extent, but there would always be instances when the fennec will fail your training, so be prepared for that.

Fennec foxes will imitate the pets of the house. If you have a dog that is litter trained, there is a higher probability that the fennec will also get better. To start the training, you can buy litter containers or boxes or pup pads. If you are buying a litter box, make sure that the box is made of paper pellets and not clay pellets. It will be more convenient for the fennec fox. The fennec's paws are covered with dense fur. If the box has clay, this will irritate his feet and will also cause abrasions. Buy a litter box that has a lid. The best way to train the pet is to buy many litter boxes. Place all these boxes in different areas of the room, so that the fennec finds one wherever he goes to relieve himself.

Slowly, remove these boxes and keep only one or two. The fennec fox should understand that he can only litter in the box. Keep one in his cage so that it is accessible. Start the training when he is still a pup. Feed him food and take him near the box, even if he doesn't want it. You should inculcate this habit in the fennec. When you see your pet going to the box on his own, give him a snack as a treat. If you find him dirtying other places, don't punish him, but just take him near his litter box. He will slowly get your point that he can only litter in the litter box. You should also make it a point to sanitize the areas that the fox has littered on. This will not allow the fennec fox to mark the place as his territory. This entire process can be hard and you would require lots of patience to train your fennec.

Clicker training

Clicker training is a process in which a sound or click is made to let the fennec fox know that something is expected from him. He should know that if he does what is expected, he will get a snack or a treat. This will motivate the fennec fox to improve his behaviour. It is important that the fennec is not punished because that will only send negative signals to his brain. You can combine the clicker training and litter training to make your fennec litter in the litter box.

Chapter 7: Ideal environment for the Fennec Fox

In the wild, the fennec fox will live under boulders and rocks. As discussed earlier, the fennec foxes dig very deep tunnels and burrows and spend most of their time there. These places are safe grounds for breeding, resting and taking care of the young ones. These tunnels can be as long as 20 feet. The fennec has the agility and strength to dig for so long. When you domesticate a fennec fox, you might find your fennec finding comfort under a chair or other piece of furniture. You will also see them to dig tunnels and holes in sand and gardens.

The ideal place for a fennec fox is indoors. The pet will feel safe and you will also be able to monitor what the pet is up to. You can also keep a cage for the pet. But, there is no need to keep him in the cage if you will be around. You can use the cage when you are sleeping or are busy with something else. An important point that needs to be noted here is that fennec foxes can't be kept in a cage for long durations. These animals are too energetic to be in the cage all the time. The animal needs to run and jump. They have too much energy in them that they need to release. If they are caged for too long, they get irritated and aggressive. They might also become unfriendly and hostile towards you. If a fennec fox is forced to be in a caged environment, he might self-mutilate in worst cases. You definitely don't want this to happen to your pet animal, so remember to cage it only when absolutely necessary.

If you are looking at an ideal temperature range for the fennec fox, then it is 60 to 80 degrees Fahrenheit. This is the temperature range that makes the fennec fox feel warm and comfortable. You should try to keep the animal inside the house at least during winters so that he does not have to bear excessive cold.

1. An indoor enclosure

There are many people who prefer to keep the fennec fox indoors. This is actually the best environment for the fennec fox. But, a lot will depend on your household and your living conditions. And, of course it won't be easy. So, you have to be prepared for the challenges that come along. This will also help you make a decision on whether you really want a fennec fox, if you still don't have one.

While you might be okay with the idea of your fennec fox staying indoors most of the time, you should also make sure that all of the other family members are also fine with this decision. The fennec fox should not be a problem for anybody. If you live in an apartment, then your neighbours might get disturbed because of the noises made by the fennec. This will be a difficult decision for you because your fennec will not stop making noises. He is a noisy pet and it is in the basic nature of the animal to be loud and extremely noisy.

As discussed earlier, a fennec is not a normal pet. You can't expect it to behave like a pet dog or cat. You should understand his characteristics and mannerisms. The fennec needs to be supervised at all times; else he will destroy things in a bid to explore stuff. To make things easier for you, you should build a cage for the fennec. You should have a provision for a cage inside the house, so that you can put the fennec in the cage when no one is around to supervise him.

Cage

Even if you plan on having an outdoor enclosure for the pet, it is imperative to have a cage inside the house. You could use it during bad weather or can use it when you want to keep the pet in front of your eyes in the house. For the indoor cage, you could use a dog crate. This would be good for the fennec fox. You should make sure that the dog crate is big and spacious. A better alternative to the dog crate is the 'ferret nation cage'. This will be spacious and ideal for the fennec fox. It is designed well and suits all the requirements of the fennec fox. You can easily purchase this cage from a store near you. You can also check for the cage online. You can expect to pay some 200 dollars to 250 dollars for this. There are different kinds of ferret cages available. A few of them have some interesting add-ons also. This is a one-time investment, so you should make sure you don't comprise on the design and construction.

While you are seeking legal help to buy the fennec fox, you should also check whether your state has any specific cage requirements. There are many states that have set very strict guidelines for the cage for various exotic animals. You can also look to buy ramp covers for the cage of the fennec foxes. These ramp covers can used to cover the ramps. This will keep the fennec's paw safe and protected.

You should furnish the inside of the cage with simple and useful things, keeping in mind the needs and requirements of the fennec fox. There should be a container for food and another one for water. You should make sure that you keep a comfortable bed inside the cage to rest when he wants to. You can also use a hammock bed if you wish to. The fennec will pass urine in the bed more often than not, so it is always a good idea to buy more than one bed and replace them in the cage when needed. You should have at least two, so that you can wash one and use the other.

It is extremely important that you clean the cage regularly. A dirty cage will only lead to infections for the fennec. You should clean the cage daily and should change the food and water in the containers provided for them. You can also keep a couple of warm blankets inside the cage. There should be a lot of toys in the cage for the fennec to play with. The fennec will play and will also bite these toys. The fennec will like snuggling to the blanket. You should try to make the cage as comfortable as possible, so that the fennec fox does not feel like a captive and starts liking the cage.

A simple trick that you can use to make the fennec fox comfortable with the cage is to instruct the fennec fox to go inside the cage, but leave the door of the cage open. If you do this, the fennec fox will also not feel captive. Let the fennec fox come out and go inside the cage at its will, but make sure that it spends considerable time in the cage. It is important the fennec fox is not forced to go into the cage. He should find the cage homely and should go there without a hesitation. This exercise should only be done under your supervision.

If you are unable to supervise the fennec fox for some reason, then don't make the mistake of keeping the cage door open. You should keep the cage door closed so that the fennec stays inside. You should always remember that no matter how much you train the fennec fox; there is a limit to how much you can trust the fennec fox. It is a hyperactive animal and will not leave any chance to do some mischief.

If you are looking at very simple yet important equipment that you can buy for the cage, get a sand box. This will allow the pet to take out his urge to dig on the sandbox. The fennec can dig as much as he wants to. But, this does not mean that he will not try to dig elsewhere. This sandbox is a way to divert him from other places and things. You should keep the sandbox at a specific position. The fennec fox will slowly learn that the sandbox is meant for it to dig. In the beginning, you can play with the pet and can act as if you are also digging in the sandbox. You will be able to purchase this sandbox for around 50 dollars. It is easily available everywhere.

As an owner, it is important for you to understand the temperament of your pet fennec. The fennec can't be kept captive for too long. This puts a negative effect on him. Even if the cage is very comfortable, make sure you bring him out. He should be allowed to release his energy by running around. This pent up energy can make him very negative and ferocious. The fox will turn sad and will only become dull with each passing day.

If you have a big house and an extra room in that house, then you can also designate one room for the pet fennec fox. The room will be like the home of the pet. He can sleep, play, eat or do whatever he wants to do in there. If you are keeping one room for the fennec fox, then you should furnish it with the right things. The rooms should be spacious and airy. There should be a lot of toys in the room for the fennec to play with. If you are looking at buying some toys for the fennec fox, then you can choose from toys such as cat climbers, cat teasers, shelves, small toys and cat towers. All these items will be a source of great amusement and fun for the fennec fox. It is also important that you fox proof this particular room.

2. An outdoor enclosure

You can also build an outdoor enclosure for your fennec. If you have figured out your indoor enclosure, then this is completely optional. You should create an outdoor enclosure only if you have the time, space and money. While an indoor enclosure does not require too much brainstorming, an outdoor enclosure will require planning. You will also be required to invest more money. If your fennec is very young, then it is best to keep him indoors. He needs the protection and love and you should also bond with him.

If you have decided to build an outdoor enclosure, then you should understand that the enclosure needs to be spacious enough to give the fennec the required area to play. The recommended size of the enclosure is 10 feet by 10 feet.

The outdoor enclosure should be planned and constructed keeping in mind the basic nature of the fennec. The animal should have fun, but should also be safe and should not get any opportunity to run away from the enclosure. The enclosure needs to be constructed with high quality material. You can look at using the chain links that are utilized to build cyclone fences. These fences are very strong and durable. There is a chance that while playing the fennec's head might just get stuck in the gap in the fence. To prevent any such accident, you can install a preventive wire, such as chicken wire, outside the main fence. This will ensure that the fennec does not get trapped when you are not around.

A fennec fox is a good climber. You have to take preventive measures so that the fennec fox does not climb out. You should make sure that the enclosure has fencing on the top area. The fennec also loves digging. It should also be taken care of that the fennec fox can't dig and eventually escape the enclosure. You should also fence the floor area of the enclosure. This will make sure that the fennec can't escape. To make things look like his natural habitat, cover the fence on the floor with sand, plants, wooden chips and twigs. You can keep the food container, water container and also the litter container over the sand. Your house should have a fencing to protect the fennec fox from stray animals. The fennec should be able to be at peace when in the enclosure. He should be able to do whatever he wants to do.

3. Fennec fox proofing

While a fennec fox can be loveable and adorable, it can also be very destructive. As the owner, it is your responsibility to bring out the best in him. If a fennec fox is forced to stay in a cage for longer durations, his destructive mind is activated. You should allow the fennec fox to feel free. But, to be able to do so, you will have fox proof your house. This means to create an environment where the fennec fox is happy and minimum damage is done to the things in the house.

If you wish to make your home suitable for the fox then you should be ready to let off certain things. You should not keep expensive carpets in areas where the fennec will play because the fennec will spoil it. Instead, make use of old rags and carpets. Fennecs get attracted to shiny things. Don't keep shiny show pieces in the house. The fennec will approach it and might destroy it or hurt himself. You should also not keep breakable things in the house.

There are certain food items that are very dangerous for the fennec. You should make sure that the pet has no access to these items. Also, make sure that all chemicals and harmful substances are not reachable to him. The fennec fox will also have a tendency to scratch the surfaces of various furniture items. Make sure that you clean the surface as soon as possible. All the electrical equipment should be kept at a safe distance from the fennec. The sockets should be covered so that the pet animal is not harmed. You should not leave any food items on the table or shelves. The fennec fox will jump and eat everything. The washroom door should always be kept closed, especially the toilet seat. There should be no wires on the floor of the house. You should also keep all the doors and windows closed to not give him a chance to escape.

Chapter 8: Common Health Issues

If proper care is given to the food served to the fennec fox, then these animals can live a healthy life without falling sick very often. The average life span for a fennec that is held captive is around 15 years. You should make sure that the fox is given his vaccines on time. Before you buy the fennec fox from the breeder, you need to discuss the animal's vaccines. All the vaccines that were not administered should be done.

Even if your pet is healthy and fine, you should take him for regular check-ups to the veterinarian. This is important so that even the smallest health issue can be tracked at an early stage. The animal can't do much on his own. His well-being and health should be your responsibility.

Though you can save your pet from the onset of diseases by taking proper care of his food and also hygiene, it is useful to know the various diseases that can affect your fennec fox. The understanding of these diseases will make you more cautious towards avoiding them in case of your fox. In general, all the diseases that can affect cats and dogs can also harm the fennec fox. The following list of various diseases that can affect a fennec fox will help you to avoid them and save your pet fennec from them:

1. **Fleas:** A very common problem that your fennec fox might suffer from is the infestation from fleas. Fleas are known to infest almost all pet animals. You should be on the look out for this. The fleas could have transmitted to the fennec fox from other pet animals in the house, such as the cats and the dogs. Your fox will be visibly irritated if its skin has been infested by the fleas. You will be able to spot small brown marks on the skin of the fox, indicating the presence of fleas. The fleas will suck the blood of the fennec, making it weak and irritable. Though this is a common problem, once detected the fleas should be removed as soon as possible.

It is always important to eliminate the actual cause of any problem. If you know that there are other pet animals in the house that are infested by fleas then it is important that you treat them all. You can use skin friendly ointments and creams to give some relief to the pet. You should also make sure that the fennec fox is being served a healthy diet so that the immune system of the animal is in place.

2. **Taurine deficiency:** Taurine deficiency is a common disease in many fennecs. The cause of this disease is the deficiency of taurine

in the diet of the pet. Taurine is very important for the overall development of the fox. Once the pet acquires this deficiency, he can develop many other complications. It is said that taurine deficiency can affect the eyesight and the heart of the animal.

To avoid this disease, it is very important that you make sure that your pet is being fed enough quantities of taurine in his daily diet. The best way to avoid this disease is by taking care of his daily diet. You can also discuss the amount of taurine that your pet fennec might need in his daily diet.

3. **Canine distemper:** Canine distemper is a disease that can be fatal if not treated on time. It is caused by a virus and it mostly affects various other animals, such as ferrets, dogs and cats. The virus that causes this disease is said to be very deadly. It is from the family paramyxovirus. It is a single strand RNA virus. It is known that this disease is one of the major reasons of mortality in young fennecs or kits. The virus affects a weak immune system. The immune system of the kits is not fully developed, so they can't survive once they are attacked by the virus. The major cause of this disease is contact with other animals that are already battling this disease. You should take special care of small fennecs so that they don't come in contact with another animal carrying the virus. The symptoms of this disease are high fever, running nose, tired and watery eyes, cough and loss of appetite. If you notice any of these symptoms then you know that your fennec needs medical attention. The sooner you get your fennec to the vet, the better.

As the owner of a fennec fox, you must know that there are vaccines available to protect your fennec fox from this deadly disease. You should make sure that the vaccine is administered to your fennec fox on time.

4. **Histoplasmosis:** This disease can be caused by a very deadly fungus. Your fennec fox might inhale the fungus and develop Histoplasmosis. This disease can be very fatal because it affects the lungs of the fennec fox. The lungs will develop complications to a point that they might stop functioning. This particular fungus is found in the various excretions of the fennec fox, such as his urine, faeces and vomit. The pet might inhale the fungus into his system and this will affect his lungs drastically. The most obvious symptom that you would notice on the onset of this disease is that the pet will have a difficulty in breathing. In severe cases, he might be found panting for breath. This is an alarming situation and a veterinarian should be consulted as soon as possible.

The necessary precaution that you need to take so that your pet fennec is saved from Histoplasmosis is to make sure that hygiene levels are maintained around the pet. The pet should never be allowed to roam around his own excretions. You should make sure that the area is cleaned as soon as the pet vomits, defecates or urinates.

5. **Pneumonia**: Your fennec fox could also be suffering from a case of pneumonia. Pneumonia in pet animals is caused by bacteria. The bacterial infection can become fatal if it is not treated at the right time. This condition can also be caused by infestation by a virus. The bacteria or the virus infects the lungs of the pet animal. Because the lungs are directly affected, the pet will face difficulty in breathing. The pet will get tired easily and will have difficulty in breathing if it runs or walks rapidly. You will also find the fennec coughing a lot. Other common symptoms include high fever, dehydration, and sudden weight loss, running nose, lethargy, watery eyes and loss of appetite. If you notice any of these symptoms then you know that your fennec needs medical attention.

You should be on the lookout for the various symptoms discussed. Consult a veterinarian if you think that your fennec might have pneumonia. He might administer certain fluids if the fennec is dehydrated. He will also suggest an antimicrobial medication that will help the fox to heal faster. Take care of the diet of the fennec. Your pet might take some time to recover fully.

6. **Corneal lesions:** A corneal lesion is a condition when the cornea of the eyes is broken or is torn apart. This condition can occur when a foreign substance disturbs the eye or enters the eye. This can also occur when some sort of a trauma has affected the eye of the pet. You should look out for any redness in the eye of the pet. The eyes might also become watery because of the infection.

This condition can be avoided by taking certain precautions. If you notice something different with the eye of the pet, make sure that you visit the veterinarian as soon as possible. It is not right to delay any matter related to sensitive areas, such as the eyes. The veterinarian might change the diet of the pet or might administer some eye drops that will give the pet some relief.

7. **Glaucoma:** The condition where the animal loses his complete eye sight is called as Glaucoma. It should be noted that this condition is irreversible, so if your pet loses his eye sight, he will never get it back. But, the process is gradual. So, you can stop the disease from spreading. The main cause behind the problem of Glaucoma is an increase in eye pressure. This increased eye pressure disturbs the

eyes of the animal to a level that his eyes start damaging. The symptoms that you should be on the lookout for are redness in the eye and decreased energy of the pet. The pet might keep bumping into things on his way because he can't see them properly.

The best way to stop the irreversible loss that the eyes can suffer is to be very sensitive towards any symptoms that you might spot. Don't overlook anything that you don't find normal. Take the pet to the veterinarian in case of any doubt. If the condition is treated well, it will not spread further.

8. **Conjunctivitis**: The inflammation of the conjunctiva is known as Conjunctivitis. Conjunctivitis is a condition when the conjunctiva of the eye is ruptured. Conjunctiva lies just below the eye lid and over the white area of the eye. Conjunctivitis can be caused by a bacterial infection or a viral infection. This condition can occur when a foreign substance disturbs the eye or enters the eye. There are many symptoms that can help you identify the onset of Conjunctivitis. You should look out for any redness in the eye of the pet. The white area of the eye would appear to be red or pink. The eyes might also become watery because of the infection. There could be a discharge from the eye also due to the viral or bacterial infection.

This condition can be avoided by taking certain precautions. Keep the eyes of the pet clean at all times. If the infection is not too severe, the eyes will recover without any treatment. If you notice something different with the eye of the pet, make sure that you visit the veterinarian as soon as possible. He will be able to diagnose the cause and will also suggest the right remedies. It is not right to delay any matter related to sensitive areas, such as the eyes. The veterinarian might administer some eye drops that will give the pet some relief.

9. **Dermatitis:** This is a skin problem and is usually caused by mites. The inflammation of the skin because of the infection caused by mites is called as Dermatitis. It is not a very deadly disease and can be controlled easily with the help of few precautions and measures. Like other pet animals, fennec foxes can also be attacked by mites easily. Once the pet acquires this disease, it keeps spreading if the condition is not treated. It is a skin disease, so a change in the texture of the skin on the pet could be an indication of an infection. In most cases, the skin starts getting red. The pet will scratch again and again at one spot. You will find the pet to be very irritated and agitated. The skin could also develop rashes or scales.

This skin disease can be treated by the use of mild medicated soaps. These soaps will soothe the skin and will also treat the infection. There are some creams that can also help to treat the skin and make the condition better. In severe cases, certain ointments might have to be applied to the skin. You should also take care of the diet of the pet. A good diet will help the skin to heal itself faster. In case the skin gets worse with passing time, then you will have to consult the veterinarian. He might suggest some oral medicines to heal the skin faster. He might also suggest some special ointments that will give some relief to the pet.

10. **Cardiomyopathy:** Another danger that can affect your fennec is cardiomyopathy. This is not a common ailment, but it is being discussed because it has affected fennec foxes in the past. Cardiomyopathy basically means that the heart tissues become dead. They stop functioning. The exact cause of the disease is not yet known.

It is extremely important that you understand that the list of diseases shared with you are for reference purpose only. This list should not scare you or make you lax when it comes to the health of your pet. It is never advisable to treat the pet at home in case of any discomfort or infection. The exhaustive list has been shared to educate you, but in case you spot any of the discussed symptoms, you should consult the veterinarian immediately. He would physically examine the pet and let you know what needs to be done. It is also important that you don't ignore any obvious symptom that your pet might be showing. There are many owners that commit this mistake of ignoring symptoms. This will only worsen the condition of the pet animal.

Chapter 9: Necessary Precautions to be Taken

If you are serious about bringing a fennec fox home, then you should understand that there are certain precautions that each owner should follow. You have to make efforts to understand the particular nature of your pet. Just like each human being is different from the other human being, each fennec fox is also unique. You have to allow yourself the time to understand the behaviour, mannerisms, habits and moods of the pet. This will allow you to take the necessary precautions to avoid unpleasant incidents for your pet fennec fox.

Though many people have started domesticating the fennec fox, it is an exotic animal by nature. So, there are a few guidelines that you should follow to keep the animal and also others around him safe. There are certain guidelines that you should follow at your home and also at public places where you might take your pet.

1. Precautions at Home

By nature, the fennec fox is very aggressive. If taken care in an appropriate manner, the animal can be very friendly, but still the basic nature of the animal can't be changed. There are a few precautions that you should follow when looking after the pet at home. These precautions will depend on the conditions of your household, whether you have children or not and whether you have other pets or not. The various scenarios and how you should take care of your pet fennec have been discussed in this section.

Precautions with Children

If you have children at home, then you need to train your children along with training the animal. The children need to be taught about the aggressive nature of the pet. Kids can sometimes pull the pet's fur when in a playful mood. The child might just trying to be a little friendly or naughty, but the fennec fox can get irritated. While many pet animals might not react to such an action, the fennec fox can't get angry and might even bite the kid.

You should keep children below the age of 5 away from the pet. The simple reason for this is that smaller kids will not understand how to behave with the pet. They will not be able to understand the specific requirements and also reactions of the pet. Even if they are under adult supervision, there are high chances of a mishap. So, in the best interest of the pet and also the child, you should keep smaller kids away from the fennec fox.

You should make sure that the older children play with the pet only under your supervision or some adult supervision. If your kid is older, you can allow him to play with the pet fox. But, you should make sure that the child understands the actions and reactions of the pet well. You should have a discussion with the kid as to how the fennec fox is different from the rest of the pets. It is important that the kid knows the pet well. You should also make sure that you don't scare your child away. You need to inform him for his own safety. But, that does not mean that he should be scared of his pet. When the kid understands how he should behave with the fennec fox, he makes it easier for himself to have a great bond with the fox.

Precautions with Other pets of the house

Fennec foxes are quite good with other pets in the house. If the fox does not sense any potential danger from the other animal in the house, he will be cordial with it. The fennec fox can have his own preferences. For example, the fennec fox is fonder of dogs than cats. A cat will also not feel very comfortable around the fox because of is high energy levels. But, the fox might not be very fond of dogs that are used for hunting.

In particular, a fennec fox will be fond of pets that it grew up with. The fox will also be fine with pets larger in size than him. If you want to have more pets in the household, make sure that they are brought around the same time and are similar in age range. This will help them to bond well. When you first introduce your pets to each other, you need to be extra cautious. In the beginning, keep the pets away from each other, but in the same vicinity so that they can identify with each other's smell.

If you have pets that are smaller in size as compared to your fennec fox, then you should keep the pets away from the fox. For example, if you have a small turtle, rabbit, bird or a rodent in the house, they need to be away from the fox for their own safety. Your fennec fox might attack the smaller pet and might try to eat it if you are not careful enough to keep them away.

It is important to note that even if the pets in the household seem friendly and cordial to each other, you should make sure that there is some supervision when they are together. You never know when they get hostile towards each other for some petty issue.

Precautions with the owner

As the owner of the wild fennec fox, you have to make sure that you take all the necessary precautions to keep everything under control. There are many obvious and necessary precautionary steps that you would need to exercise.

You should take efforts to make sure that all the safety precautions are taken. The enclosure should be built keeping in mind all the necessary safety measures. Apart from these measures, you would also have to take certain precautions as the owner of the fox.

Fennec foxes are very fast. They will run from a point to another within a split of a second. You might face many difficulties tracing the pet and keeping a track of where he is. As the owner, it is important that you are aware of your pet's whereabouts at all times. This will allow you to know if the pet is up to some mischief or not.

Another issue that you can face is that the fennec fox can step on a smaller pet while running around. This is a serious matter and you should look for ways to avoid such situations. You should keep the smaller pets as far as possible from the fennec fox. Another simple thing that you can do is to tie a collar around the fox's neck. You should also make sure that this collar has a few bells. This will help you to know where the fennec fox is because as he moves around, the bells will ring.

As the owner of the fennec fox, you have to be well prepared. Not all fennec foxes are the same, so this makes your task more challenging. When you bring your pet home, start out very slowly with him. Look for his reactions for everything that you do. This will help you to understand what your pet enjoys and what he does not enjoy.

It is known that many fennec foxes can get irritated by a rub on their belly. You will have to find out if this is true for your pet fennec fox or not. Try to give slight rubs on the belly in the beginning and look out for his reactions. An important point that you should note is that you should never force your pet to do anything. If he does not enjoy a belly rub, there should be no reason for you to force the rubs on him. Allow him to enjoy what he genuinely enjoys.

When your pet is very young, start out with rubbing around his ears. Make sure that you are as gentle as possible. You shouldn't hurt the pet in any way. Slowly rub other parts of his body. But, each time you try something new, look for the pet's reactions. If you think that he is not enjoying himself then avoiding petting those particular areas.

Precautions with Guests in the house

If you are having guests at your place, then you should make sure that the guests are not allowed to pet the fennec fox. There are many fennec foxes that are friendly towards complete strangers, but there are many who will want to stay away. If your pet is in a habit to socialize from the beginning, he grows up to be cordial towards strangers.

The nature of the fox will depend on how you have raised him, but in general a fennec fox is not very good with strangers. If the guests try to get extremely pushy on the fennec fox, he might even try to bite them. A fennec fox bites when he is scared. It is like a defence mechanism for him.

There is another defence mechanism that the fox can use. A fennec fox is known to release a violent gland when it is in a state of fear. The odour of the violent gland can be quite unbearable for you and your guests. To save your guests from such incidents, ask them to stay away from the pet.

If you and your guests are around the fennec fox, try not to encroach upon his space. Just leave him alone. In such a case, the fennec fox will not acknowledge the presence of the guests and will be on his own. If you know that your pet will get disturbed and agitated, it is better to keep him in the cage till your guests are around.

You should also understand that each fennec fox will have a unique personality. It will depend on how you have raised him and also on his unique characteristic. There are some fennec foxes that love being around people, while there are many others who turn out to be very shy. As you raise your fox, make efforts to understand the unique personality of your fennec fox. This will help you to understand how to deal with him.

2. Precautions at Public places

You might be contemplating on the idea to take your pet fennec fox to public places, but before you can do that, it is important to understand your pet well. A fennec fox can be very unpredictable in a public place, so it becomes all the more important to take the necessary precautions and safety measures. This is important so that the pet and also other people around him are safe and sound.

Before you take out your fennec fox out, it is imperative that you understand the various situations that you can encounter. This will help you to be better prepared and well equipped for the situation.

Your fennec fox will run away at the first opportunity that it gets. You might love your pet and your pet might be very devoted towards you, but you should know that you can't expect your fennec fox to be very loyal. They can never be as loyal as a dog. So, you have to be very careful and be prepared for this particular aspect. Don't leave your pet unsupervised under any circumstances. Even when you are around the pet in an open space, make sure that the fennec fox gets no chance to escape. They will just grab any opportunity that they get to run away. Make sure that you don't provide them this opportunity.

When you take your fennec fox outside, the pet is guaranteed to get a lot of attention. Because of the way they look, the fennec foxes will get a lot of human attention. People might want to touch them, pet them and play with them, without realizing how aggressive these animals can be. As an owner, it is your responsibility that you don't allow strangers to touch the pet fox. You should know that your fennec fox will not enjoy strangers to be touching him. He would like to be petted only the way he enjoys it. With too many strangers around things might get out of control. He might get irritated by people touching him, and he might just end up biting people.

You have to remember that you are domesticating a wild exotic animal. The government rules for your exotic pet will be very different from the rules for other normal pets. Your fennec fox can also be euthanized if he bites people. People might complain against the fennec fox, and your fennec fox might be left at the mercy of the decision that the authorities take for him. This is a serious issue and you should avoid getting into such circumstances as any cost.

A fennec fox is very small in size and so they don't appear very frightening. They look nice, and generally people will love the sight of a fennec fox. But, if the fox gets into an unpleasant incident, then the people around you will raise objections of the owning of an exotic animal. You will find it more and more difficult to take the animal outside.

If you will be in an open space for a long time, you can build a temporary enclosure for your fennec fox in the open space. This will ensure that the pet has his space and is happy. He can run around, play and enjoy the weather also. And, you can rest assured that the pet is happy, safe and is not running away anywhere.

Conclusion

Thank you for purchasing this book!

I hope this book was able to help you in understanding the various ways to domesticate and care for fennec foxes.

The fennec fox is an exotic animal. Many people find them adorable and wish to domesticate them. In earlier times, the fennec fox was only found in the wild, but now many people have started domesticating these animals. But, even now there are many things that these prospective owners don't understand about the fennec fox. They find themselves getting confused as to what should be done and what should be avoided. If you are one of those people who wish to raise a fennec fox as a pet, there are many things that you need to keep in mind. You should be able to understand everything about the fennec before you buy one. You need to make sure that you are ready in terms of the right preparation.

You can't just go and buy a fennec fox. You have to be sure that you can provide for the animal. So, it is important to be acquainted with the dos and don'ts of keeping the fennec. You can only make a wise decision when you are acquainted with all these and more. When you are planning to domesticate a fennec fox as a pet, you should lay special emphasis on its diet requirements, common health issues and breeding styles.

When you bring a pet home, it becomes your responsibility to raise the pet in the best way possible. You have to provide physically, mentally, emotionally and financially for the pet. Before you embark on this journey of raising your pet, it is important to evaluate your resources and make sure that you are ready for the pet.

Fennec foxes are very different from the other foxes. They are unique in many of their characteristics. As pets, fennec foxes can be adorable, independent, entertaining and lovable. But, they need to be taken care of. They have certain specific requirements that need to be met. You have to understand their specific requirements before you can adopt them. This will help you to hand raise the animal in the best possible way. You should provide the animal with the right shelter, right food and the right health care facilities. This will help you to form a great bond with your fennec fox.

The ways and strategies discussed in the book are meant to help you get acquainted with everything that you need to know about fennec foxes. You will be able to appreciate all the qualities of the fennec fox that make him suitable to be a household pet. The book teaches you simple ways that will help you to understand your pet fennec. This will allow you take care of your pet in a better way. You should be able to appreciate your pet and also care well for the fennec fox as your pet with the help of this book.

Thank you and good luck!

References

http://www.nationalgeographic.com

www.ehow.co.uk

http://www.mnn.com

http://www.arkive.org

http://animals.sandiegozoo.org

www.bbc.co.uk

https://www.cuteness.com

https://www.thespruce.com

http://fennecfoxes.net

http://crittercamp.weebly.com

https://en.wikipedia.org

http://www.arkive.org

http://exoticanimalsforsale.net

www.environment.nsw.gov.au

www.wildlifeontheweb.co.uk

www.training.ntwc.org

www.wildlifehealth.org

http://animaldiversity.org

https://www.yourpetspace.info

https://www.finecomb.com

http://www.iucnredlist.org

https://a-z-animals.com

https://www.theguardian.com

https://animalcorner.co.uk

http://www.zooborns.typepad.com

https://www.stlzoo.org

http://www.wildlifelearningcenter.org

https://nationalzoo.si.edu

http://www.lpzoo.org

Copyright and Trademarks: This publication is Copyrighted 2017 by IMB Publishing. All products, publications, software and services mentioned and recommended in this publication are protected by trademarks. In such instance, all trademarks & copyright belong to the respective owners. All rights reserved. No part of this book may be reproduced or transferred in any form or by any means, graphic, electronic, or mechanical, including photocopying, recording, taping, or by any information storage retrieval system, without the written permission of the authors. Pictures used in this book are either royalty free pictures bought from stock-photo websites or have the source mentioned underneath the picture.

Disclaimer and Legal Notice: This product is not legal or medical advice and should not be interpreted in that manner. You need to do your own due-diligence to determine if the content of this product is right for you. The author and the affiliates of this product are not liable for any damages or losses associated with the content in this product. While every attempt has been made to verify the information shared in this publication, neither the author nor the affiliates assume any responsibility for errors, omissions or contrary interpretation of the subject matter herein. Any perceived slights to any specific person(s) or organization(s) are purely unintentional. We have no control over the nature, content and availability of the web sites listed in this book. The inclusion of any web site links does not necessarily imply a recommendation or endorse the views expressed within them. IMB Publishing takes no responsibility for, and will not be liable for, the websites being temporarily unavailable or being removed from the Internet. The accuracy and completeness of information provided herein and opinions stated herein are not guaranteed or warranted to produce any particular results, and the advice and strategies, contained herein may not be suitable for every individual. The author shall not be liable for any loss incurred as a consequence of the use and application, directly or indirectly, of any information presented in this work. This publication is designed to provide information in regards to the subject matter covered. The information included in this book has been compiled to give an overview of the subject s and detail some of the symptoms, treatments etc. that are available to people with this condition. It is not intended to give medical advice. For a firm diagnosis of your condition, and for a treatment plan suitable for you, you should consult your doctor or consultant. The writer of this book and the publisher are not responsible for any damages or negative consequences following any of the treatments or methods highlighted in this book. Website links are for informational purposes and should not be seen as a personal endorsement; the same applies to the products detailed in this book. The reader should also be aware that although the web links included were correct at the time of writing, they may become out of date in the future.

www.ingramcontent.com/pod-product-compliance
Lightning Source LLC
Chambersburg PA
CBHW060851050426
42453CB00008B/930